Havana

Before CASTRO

EXOTIC EXCITING ENCHANTING ENTRANCING

CUBA
BY FLYING CLIPPER

PAN AMERICAN WORLD AIRWAYS
The System of the Flying Clippers

Havana

FACING:
Castro and his victorious rebels in January 1959.

RIGHT:
Early Habana Hilton rendering from 1956.

Before CASTRO

When Cuba Was a Tropical Playground

PETER MORUZZI

GIBBS SMITH

TO ENRICH AND INSPIRE HUMANKIND

Salt Lake City | Charleston | Santa Fe | Santa Barbara

First Edition
12 11 10 09 08   5 4 3 2 1

Text © 2008 Peter Moruzzi

Published by
Gibbs Smith
P.O. Box 667
Layton, Utah 84041

Orders: 1.800.835.4993
www.gibbs-smith.com

Designed by Kurt Wahlner
Printed and bound in China

Library of Congress Cataloging-in-Publication Data

Moruzzi, Peter.
  Havana before Castro : when Cuba was a tropical playground / Peter Moruzzi. — 1st ed.
      p. cm.
  Includes bibliographical references and index.
  ISBN-13: 978-1-4236-0367-2
  ISBN-10: 1-4236-0367-2
 1. Havana (Cuba)—Description and travel. 2. Havana (Cuba)—Social life and customs—20th century. I. Title.
  F1799.H34M67 2008
  972.9106'3—dc22
                                    2008008152

PAGE ONE:
Pan Am's Flying Clipper to Cuba brochure from 1947.

LEFT:
Pensylvania Club drink menu from 1940.

Contents

Preface

What began in 1987 with the discovery of a tattered brochure buried among ephemera in a Fort Lauderdale antiques shop led to an intermittent two-decade inquiry into Cuba's pre-Castro past. The brochure was for the Tropicana, a name I associated with Ricky Ricardo's nightclub and the Las Vegas hotel of the same name. However, this Tropicana was not in the United States but in 1950s Cuba. Opening the brochure revealed color renderings of "Lefty Clark's New Casino," the "Under the Stars Terrace," and, most fascinating of all, the ultramodern "Crystal Arch Room." Being an aficionado of modern architecture and an avid student of Las Vegas's mob-related history, the combination of both modernism and gambling depicted in a luxuriant tropical setting was a revelation.

In particular, I was interested in the Havana of the 1940s and 1950s. What was the city like at that time and why was it so popular with Americans? Why had the Afro-Cuban rumba, mambo, and cha-chá become so wildly popular at America's snazziest ballrooms and nightclubs before and after the Second World War? How accurate was the depiction of Batista's Havana as a debauched, mafia-infested, pre-revolutionary powder keg as portrayed in *The Godfather Part II*? Did the dictator actually flee the coun-

try on New Year's Eve, followed by the country's rich and powerful? What happened to all of the vibrant bars, restaurants, nightclubs, and cabarets—considered the most fabulous in the world—after Castro took over?

Later, as an architectural historian, I became fascinated with Havana's architectural legacy—its colonial and neocolonial heritage, its Art Deco and Streamline Moderne designs, and, closest to my heart, the city's wealth of incredible Modern buildings constructed after World War II. As with such inquiries, the deeper I dug, the wider became my interest. The answers that I found led to the writing of this book, which attempts to explore Havana from the perspective of an American tourist visiting the city during the first half of the twentieth century and, many decades later, as a twenty-first-century tourist intent on rediscovering the city's astonishing past.

LEFT:
The 1957 Tropicana brochure that sparked the author's obsession with pre-Castro Havana.

RIGHT:
Entrance to L'aiglon dining room at Meyer Lansky's Havana Riviera in 2007.

Acknowledgments

After years of researching and writing the story of pre-Castro Havana, it is an honor to acknowledge those whose efforts, inspiration, and guidance helped bring my approach to the subject to life. It is with profound and heartfelt appreciation that I embrace my intrepid fellow explorers Sven Kirsten and Naomi Alper along with our guides Andrés and Arturo. Together we doggedly traversed the city's highlights and lowlights in search of its furtive past. Indeed, it is due to Sven's astonishing photographic eye that Havana's multilayered history is revealed in this book. In addition, as the undisputed Big Kahuna of Polynesian Pop and author of *The Book of Tiki* and *Tiki Modern,* Sven provided the sidebar about the peculiar tale of the Habana Hilton's Trader Vic's. Another friend, the world expert on historic tropical mixology and author of *Sippin' Safari,* Jeff Berry, provided the stories behind the six vintage Cuban cocktails, along with their recipes, featured in this book.

Thanks to Chris Nichols for inspiring me to authorhood and for introducing me to the supportive and enthusiastic publisher Gibbs Smith; to Eduardo Luis Rodríguez for pioneering the rediscovery, research, and documentation of Cuba's astounding modern architectural heritage; to James McQuaid, the irrepressible creative force responsible for the furnishings and interior design of the Habana Hilton; and to Bruce Becket as the keeper of his father's architectural legacy.

Thanks also to Joan Harrison for editing my early manuscript and helping to clarify my vision; to my editor Jared Smith for his professionalism, keen eye, and patience in dealing with an impatient author; to Rosa Lowinger and Ophelia Fox, who brought the luminosity of Tropicana in the 1950s to life; to Robert Lacey for his exhaustive portrait of the rise and fall of Meyer Lansky; to historian and author Rosalie Schwartz for her groundbreaking research into mass tourism in pre-Castro Cuba; to Isabel Ezquerra, librarian and archivist of the University of Miami's Cuban Heritage Collection; and to Bruce Emerton, architectural research librarian extraordinaire.

My gratitude goes to fellow collector Vincent Martino Jr., whose obsession with midcentury Cuba mirrored my own; to eBay as the twenty-first-century source for many of the world's concealed treasures; to *Stag* and *Cabaret* magazines of the 1950s for documenting Havana's well-known, but rarely depicted, seedy underbelly; and to *Cigar Aficionado* magazine for its ongoing celebration of Cuban cigars. To the wizard of graphic design, Kurt Wahlner, who transformed a mass of text and images into the book that I had always envisioned, I raise a toast—the El Presidente cocktail, in fact—for his extraordinary efforts. To my father for instilling in me a sense of adventure and a restless curiosity that continues to propel me forward, and to my mother for her gentle spirit, who, as a lifelong vocal performer, encouraged me to share my passions with the world—I am profoundly grateful.

Finally, my eternal thanks to my life partner Lauren LeBaron, whose endless patience, support, and unqualified love made this project possible.

THE TROPICAL HOLIDAY ISLE

ABOVE:
Vacuum-cleaner sales-man/British agent Jim Wormold (Alec Guinness) is served poisoned daiquiris in *Our Man in Havana* in 1959.

Havana's American businessmen and the mobsters running the big casinos had a tin ear when it came to Cuba's rapidly growing guerilla movement in 1958. Their blind confidence in Batista's ability to suppress the island's spreading social and political turbulence was astonishing considering the enormous financial investments that they had made in the country. Such naiveté was reinforced by the American embassy's failure to accurately gauge the escalating guerilla threat and preemptively warn American business interests of the mounting dangers.

Since the beginning of 1958, Castro's strength and reputation had grown in counterpoint with the inability of Batista's forces to rout the guerillas from their mountain camps in the Sierra Maestra. As a result, urban students fleeing Batista's brutal repression increasingly joined impoverished rural peasants in the guerillas' mountain redoubt. While middle-class Habaneros were equally exhausted with Batista's repression and the country's increasing instability, most went about their daily activities with the hope that things would improve when a new government finally replaced Batista's brutal kleptocracy.

In the propaganda battle, Castro's revolutionary movement had been given an important boost by a series of adulatory *New York Times* articles written by Herbert L. Matthews in 1957. Charmed by Castro's magnetism and convinced of his egalitarian zeal, Matthews, who endured the arduous trek to the rebel's secret mountain camp, was convinced that Castro and his bearded revolutionaries constituted a righteous and formidable threat to Cuba's corrupt dictatorship. The correspondent's impassioned dispatches left readers with the impression that Castro and his rebels were a larger and more threatening guerilla force than they actually were. Indeed, the articles had the effect of validating the budding romantic myth of Castro as a selfless freedom fighter who, with his bedraggled but valiant comrades, was willing to perform any sacrifice to free Cuba of the hated Batista and restore democracy to its people.

Fanning out from the Sierra Maestra in late 1958, Castro's growing revolutionary army routed Batista's forces in several villages and towns in the country's eastern provinces. These victories had the compound effect of demoralizing the army and increasing Castro's renown as a revolutionary leader.

As New Year's Eve 1958 approached, Havana's burgeoning middle class looked warily toward the coming year. Yet mobsters Meyer Lansky and Santo Trafficante Jr., Tropicana Nightclub owner Martin Fox, the new managers of the Habana Hilton, and the many shopkeepers, bar owners, musicians, small-time hustlers, and tens of thousands of white-collar professionals isolated in steamy Havana were nonetheless unprepared for the surging tidal wave that was about to wash them all away.

Introduction

Whether a weekend package tourist or a traveler who becomes immersed in the local culture, one's experience of a city is inextricably tied to the background circumstances of its history. Consequently, in order to get a sense of what it was like to be an American visiting Havana before the revolution, an overview of Cuban history is especially helpful, from its evolution as a Spanish colony to its place in the Americas as the zenith of passion and vice, musical achievement and architectural splendor, and political corruption and revolutionary fervor.

Initial chapters in this book document Cuba's Spanish colonial period, from discovery by Columbus in 1492 to occupation by American forces in 1898, a time when Cuba was one of Spain's most prized New World possessions due to its strategic position in the Caribbean and the riches it produced. Havana, the island's capital city, benefited from the construction of beautiful colonial architectural wonders—forts, churches, mansions, administrative buildings—that remain treasures of great national pride today. Such wonders came at a terrible cost, however, as the city's assets were built on the backs of hundreds of thousands of captured slaves imported to work the island's vast fields of sugarcane.

In the decades leading to America's victory in the Spanish–American war of 1898 and its occupation of Cuba, the United States repeatedly sought to purchase or annex the nearby island for its wealth, scenic beauty, and charms of lovely Havana. Thus, to ensure that Cuban independence in 1902 would not mean the end of American influence, the notorious Platt Amendment was ratified to guarantee the right of American intervention in Cuba's affairs at the discretion of Uncle Sam. Under the umbrella of American power, the Cuban republic was cursed by a parade of inept and corrupt presidents that culminated in the dictatorship of Fulgencio Batista in the 1950s. Yet historic images reveal that governmental avarice benefited the city of Havana, which was the recipient of graft-laden public works projects such as the construction of the presidential palace, the capitol building, Fifth Avenue in suburban Miramar, and the Hotel Nacional.

The discovery of Havana in the 1920s by America's wealthy led to it becoming their winter playground with the establishment of country clubs and racetracks, a national casino, yacht clubs, golf courses, and suburban mansions. At the same time, other Americans arrived in Havana simply to escape Prohibition and enjoy a cocktail at Sloppy Joe's Bar with impunity and, at the same time, experience the city's romantic foreignness or, perhaps, its notorious reputation as a "goddess of delights."

While the Great Depression of the 1930s put a damper on American tourism to the island, Cuban culture, particularly its music and dance, had a great impact on the United States. Starting with the rumba and the Cuban bandleaders and singers who made it famous—from Xavier Cugat to Desi Arnaz—Cuban music and dance inevitably led to a desire to visit the genre's musical source, Havana. Combined with low-cost sea and air travel after World War II, Havana suddenly became the "exotic" destination of choice for hundreds of thousands of Americans excited to see the land of Babalu. In addition to music, what awaited the tourist throngs were dozens of cabarets and nightclubs unlike those found anywhere in the world. At the apex were the Big Three—Montmartre, Sans Souci, and Tropicana—with reputations for late-night extravagance that attracted tourists from suburban Cleveland to Beverly Hills.

Due to its freewheeling reputation and welcoming attitude toward foreign investment in tourism—especially during the Batista years—elements of the American mob successfully set up shop in Havana in the 1950s, taking over nightclubs, opening casinos, and building high-rise hotel resorts rivaling those of Las Vegas and Miami Beach in their over-the-top extravagance. Indeed, it was due to the prominence of Meyer Lansky's Havana Riviera, Santo Trafficante Jr.'s Sans Souci and Hotel Capri casinos, and the more legitimate Hilton Hotels International with their magnificent Habana Hilton that the city came to represent, to Americans at least, a playground of unrestrained desire.

Meanwhile, the average Havana resident (or Habanero) went about his or her daily life despite a backdrop of increasing instability and unrest. As white-collar professionals and businessmen prospered during the postwar years, they commissioned talented local architects to design residential and commercial buildings that reflected a Cuban Modernism unique to the topography and climate of the island nation. Much of this remarkable architectural legacy still exists for us to appreciate today.

In the revolutionary interregnum between New Year's Eve 1958 and today, much has changed in the Pearl of the Antilles. The goal of this book is to illustrate what made Havana the object of desire for Americans during the sixty years between the Spanish–American War and Castro's triumph, and to serve as a guide for contemporary visitors intent on locating and experiencing what remains of the city's incredible mid-century past.

From Spanish Colony to Cuban Republic

"As the yellow patched sails fluttered down their spars and the harsh clank of anchor chains broke the peace of that sunny October day in 1492, Cuba made her first conquest of white men's hearts. Since then, this gorgeous siren of the Caribbean has lured millions of earth's children across the seas within the spell of her languorous beauty. More than four centuries of passion and peace, misery and contentment have taught her wisdom. She has become cultured in the arts of civilization—in short, a charming modern. Yet, despite the brilliance of her sophistication, she still nourishes the fires of her untamed youth, the provocative beauty that always lived in the memory of Columbus and moved him to declare to his royal patrons, 'The loveliest land that human eyes have ever seen.'"

— "Cuba" brochure published by the Cuban National Tourist Commission, circa 1931

RIGHT:
Rough Rider Teddy Roosevelt leads the charge up Santiago de Cuba's San Juan Hill in the only major battle of the Spanish–American War.

When Christopher Columbus encountered the Caribbean island of Cuba in 1492, he thought that he had at last reached the Asian mainland, not the balmy isle that would become known as the "Pearl of the Antilles." Other Europeans soon followed, including Sebastián de Ocampo, who, in 1508, circumnavigated Cuba, proving that it was an island. Cuba was already populated by the Taino and Siboney Indians, the former being led by the warrior Hatuey in their struggle against the Spanish conquerors. After several protracted battles, Hatuey (who was immortalized in the

twentieth century as a brand of Cuban beer) was captured in 1512 and burned at the stake. The following year, Juan Ponce de León's futile Caribbean search for the fountain of youth brought him to an island he named "La Florida" after the flowers he found there. As we know, Florida turned out to be not an island but the North American mainland. Ponce de León's efforts were commemorated 425 years later at Havana's La Florida bar/restaurant, where he was depicted celebrating the discovery of the daiquiri, the true fountain of eternal youth.

Havana was established as a small Spanish settlement in 1514, but the port city would not become the island's capital until Santiago de Cuba relinquished the title in 1607. Prior to the disappearance of Cuba's native peoples due to Spanish brutality and European diseases, the Indians had introduced the colonists to the pleasures of tobacco, which, along with sugarcane and, later, rum, would become the island's signature commodities. By 1527, the elimination of Cuba's native population led Spain to bring the first of hundreds of thousands of African slaves to the island to toil in its burgeoning agricultural plantations. For the next three and a half centuries, Spain would regard Cuba as one of its most prized New World possessions and jealously guard the island from the French, English, Americans, and buccaneers who coveted its bountiful assets. The

BELOW LEFT:
Executed Taíno Indian leader Hatuey later became a brand of Cuban beer.

BELOW:
Ponce de León discovers the fountain of youth at the La Florida bar.

PONCE DE LEON DISCOVERING IN THE "LA FLORIDA BAR" THE FOUNTAIN OF ETERNAL YOUTH

HABANA: CASTILLO DEL MORRO

MORRO CASTLE

52557

CLOCKWISE FROM LEFT:
Obispo Street was the center of Havana's colonial shopping district. Morro Castle, built in 1589, guards Havana harbor. Columbus's remains were once located in the baroque Cathedral of San Cristóbal in Old Havana (Havana Vieja).

construction in 1589 of Morro Castle, a large stone fortress at the mouth of Havana harbor, was part of this defensive strategy. Its picturesque profile became the symbol of tourist Havana in the twentieth century.

During the long colonial period, riches from the sugar trade led to the construction of Havana's cathedral and cherished collection of baroque and neoclassical mansions, administrative buildings, warehouses, and shops crowded along narrow streets. Now known as Havana Vieja (Old Havana), this astoundingly intact colonial quarter is today's tourist magnet, having been declared a UNESCO World Heritage Site in 1982.

By the mid-1800s, Cuban nationalists such as Carlos Manuel de Céspedes, Antonio Maceo, and Máximo Gómez reacted to Spain's long dominance by engaging in a series of uprisings that led to thirty years of horrific wars of independence. During this period, Spain finally abolished slavery. In 1895, Cuban poet and independence leader José Martí was killed by Spanish troops during the Battle of Dos Ríos, becoming the country's most revered martyr and a symbol of Cuban patriotism to this day. The United States, outraged over reports of Spanish atrocities printed in the incendiary tabloid newspapers of William Randolph Hearst, sent the USS *Maine* to Havana harbor in 1898 to protect American interests and, more importantly, to intimidate the Spanish forces. Once there, the *Maine* promptly exploded, providing the pretext for America's declaration of war against Spain under the

4009. Wharf Scene, Havana, Cuba

STREET VENDOR, HAVANA, CUBA

OUTSIDE LEFT: Cuba's most revered independence leader and martyr José Martí.

ABOVE LEFT: A busy wharf scene.

LEFT: The colonial quarter's narrow streets.

BELOW: Military commander Máximo Gómez led Cuba's fight against Spain.

LEFT:
The U.S.S. *Maine* in 1898.

BELOW:
The *Maine* explodes in Havana harbor, precipitating the Spanish–American War.

BELOW RIGHT:
Lieutenant Colonel Teddy Roosevelt (center with glasses) and his Rough Riders.

battle cry "Remember the *Maine!*" Lieutenant Colonel Teddy Roosevelt's volunteer cavalry unit, known as the Rough Riders, engaged in a well-publicized charge up San Juan Hill in Santiago de Cuba that became the propaganda pinnacle of the Spanish-American War. It was a war that lasted only four months, ending with Spain's surrender. The battle made Teddy Roosevelt a hero, propelling him to the presidency and inaugurating a new century of American adventurism abroad.

Rather than independence, however, Cuba faced a four-year period of American occupation. While the country was under the authority of Governor General Leonard A. Wood, Havana's famous seaside Malecón was constructed in addition to other improvements to the city's infrastructure. In 1901,

Congress passed the imperialistic Platt Amendment, which specified the terms under which American troops would leave Cuba—but which also allowed U.S. intervention in Cuban affairs whenever the U.S. deemed it necessary. In addition, the amendment included the long-term lease of Guantanamo Bay to the United States—a lease that could be revoked only with the consent of both parties.

On May 20, 1902, in an elaborate palace ceremony, General Wood delivered President Teddy Roosevelt's letter declaring Cuba's independence and the establishment of the Republic of Cuba.

Cuba's first elected president, Tomás Estrada Palma, served until 1906, when an insurrection led American troops to reoccupy the country for another three

CLOCKWISE FROM LEFT: Governor General Leonard Wood (center, in uniform) declares Cuba's independence from the United States on May 20, 1902; Tomás Estrada Palma, Cuba's first elected president, is third left from Wood. Cuban stamp showing president Tomás Estrada Palma. Cigar box label celebrating Cuban and American friendship. Matchbook from Guantanamo Bay (G'TMO) Naval Base. Swank G'TMO officers' club.

Cuba Libre

At the dawn of the twentieth century, United States soldiers fighting the Spanish-American War in Cuba brought with them a new American beverage called Coca-Cola. It didn't take long for the locals to figure out that a shot of rum and a squeeze of lime improved the Yankee soft drink considerably. The Cuba Libre got its name after the defeat of Spain and the advent of "Free Cuba" in 1902; the drink got a leg up in the States during Prohibition, since Coke successfully masked the taste of even the most rotgut bootlegged rum. With the Andrews Sisters' 1945 hit song "Rum and Coca-Cola," the Cuba Libre entered the pantheon of famous midcentury mixed drinks. This recipe comes to us from the 1956 *Esquire Drink Book*, edited by Frederick A. Birmingham.

—Jeff Berry

Cuba Libre

1/2 ounce fresh lime juice
2 ounces white rum
2 dashes Angostura bitters
Coca-Cola

Pour lime juice and rum into a tall glass packed with crushed ice. Add bitters. Fill with Coke. Stir well.

OFFICERS CLUB NAVAL STATION GTMO. BAY CUBA.

The Prado Then and Now

L E F T : Palatial residences along Havana's Prado promenade circa 1905.

R I G H T : The same view in 2007.

FAR LEFT: Fifth Avenue in the exclusive Miramar district circa 1920.

LEFT: Upscale residences in Vedado circa 1910.

years under the terms of the Platt Amendment. Home rule returned to Cuba in 1909 with the presidency of José Miguel Gómez and the beginning of a half-century of misrule by a parade of regrettable presidents of infrequent accomplishments and varying degrees of bluster, ineptitude, and corruption.

In the first decade of the new republic, Havana's nouveau riche chose Havana Centro (central Havana) to erect their grand mansions and civic buildings, such as those lining the Prado promenade. Simultaneous with Havana Centro's growth, the previously off-limits district of adjacent El Vedado was opened for suburban development. It would be in Vedado where, during the 1950s, Havana's chicest nightclubs, cabarets, ultramodern hotels, and mob-run casinos would materialize.

The boom years of the 1920s allowed president-cum-dictator Gerardo Machado to commission the construction of the nation's central highway and inaugurate Fifth Avenue—the wide landscaped thoroughfare that went through Havana's posh seaside Miramar neighborhood to Marianao, location of the Havana country club, Jockey Club Racetrack, and Gran Casino Nacional. Before fleeing to Miami in 1933, Machado succeeded in bankrupting the treasury with the $20 million cost of his

ABOVE:
Ornate Gallego Palace was built as a Galician emigrants' social club in 1915.

LEFT:
Strolling the seaside Malecón circa 1905.

new Capitolio Nacional (National Capitol Building), with its marble halls and fifty-six-foot-high bronze Statue of the Republic that resembles a Roman goddess.

America's looming presence, meanwhile, was never far from the action—whether based upon the threat (or promise) of military intervention or with its dominance of key sectors of the Cuban economy, including the sugar industry, railroads, shipping, nickel extraction, and telecommunications. Enterprises such as the United Fruit Company, Cuban American Telephone and Telegraph, Goodyear, and Westinghouse were major players whose powerful influence in Cuban affairs was undeniable.

And in the countryside, despite picture postcards depicting rural life as quaint and charming with simple *campesinos* (farmers) posing near their *bohios* (thatch shacks), extreme levels of rural poverty eventually would drive the campesinos to unite with Castro's revolutionary forces in overthrowing the old order and, in particular, the concentration of Cuba's wealth in Havana and its suburbs.

HABANA. CAPITOLIO (DE NOCHE). CAPITOL BUILDING (BY NIGHT)

4049-29

COUNTRY HUT.

Cuba,
Donde nace el rio Almeno

FACING, LEFT:
President Machado bankrupted the treasury in commissioning the National Capitol Building in 1929.

FACING, RIGHT:
The Capitolio's over-the-top extravagance.

TOP:
A picturesque *bohio.*

ABOVE:
Living the simple life along the Almendares River.

RIGHT:
The Cuban Tourist Commission promoted a romanticized view of rural life.

Sugar, Rum, and Cigars

ABOVE:
Cuban cigar brands often were named after characters from European literature.

RIGHT:
Relaxing with a bottle of Bacardi's Hatuey beer.

Rum and cigars—hypnotic words that for most of the twentieth century evoked tropical Cuba in American minds. While tourists may have focused on Cuba's more beguiling commodities, it was actually raw sugar that dominated Cuba's economy as it had for generations. In the 1800s, the island became the world's largest sugar producer, thanks to slavery and improvements in refining technology and transportation. In addition, French

FLYING TO HEAVEN
WITH BACARDI

MADE IN CUBA

COMPAÑIA LITOGRÁFICA DE LA HABANA.

Bacardi. The company's famous bat logo dates from that year, when Facundo and his brother José began distilling vats of molasses in an old building that had fruit bats in its rafters. In 1926, the Bacardi family's third generation expanded its empire by introducing the Hatuey beer brand, which soon became Cuba's most popular. By 1930, when Havana's Art Deco masterpiece, the Bacardi Building, was erected, the company dominated the rum business. Castro's victory, however, ended ninety-eight years of Bacardi presence in Cuba when their assets were nationalized and the family fled to Miami, Puerto Rico, and Bermuda.

For American tourists a major attraction was a visit to

CLOCKWISE FROM LEFT: During Prohibition, Uncle Sam catches a lift from the Bacardi bat to rum-soaked Cuba. Havana's magnificent 1930 Art Deco Bacardi Building in 2007. 1950s-era coaster. A man's priorities. Harmonizing to Bacardi and seltzer in the 1940s. 1920s Bacardi executives celebrating another good year, with the company's history illustrated behind them.

Havana's distilleries, cellars, and tasting rooms. Photos of snockered *Norteamericanos* elbowing a clutch of rum bottles were taken to commemorate the midafternoon bingeing—a pastime frowned upon back home.

And what went best with rum? Cigars! While never approaching sugar exports in monetary value, Cuban tobacco had long been acclaimed for its rich flavor derived from the unique quality of the island's fertile soil and climate. In particular, the red earth of the Pinar del Río region situated west of Havana continues to produce the world's best tobacco. Centering Pinar del Río is the picturesque Viñales Valley, where soaring limestone outcroppings punctuate a flat plain of sweeping tobacco fields. Only a three-hour drive

ABOVE:
Living it up at the Vinatera Distillery in 1957.

RIGHT:
A quiet afternoon at the Ron Pinin tasting room in the 1930s.

from Havana, Viñales remains one of the country's must-see destinations.

In the days when "smoking a Havana" meant smoking a cigar, there were dozens of Cuban cigar brands representing distinct blends of tobacco as perfected by master cigar makers. It wasn't until the 1930s that cigarettes surpassed cigars in worldwide popularity, signaling the decline of what had once been an enormous industry employing tens of thousands. In its attempt to prop up the industry, Cuba's National Commission for Propaganda and Defense of Havana Tobacco was relentless in its promotion of

VALLE VIÑALES, CUBA. I VIÑALES VALLEY (ca)

CLOCKWISE FROM LEFT:
Harvesting tobacco in Pinar del Río circa 1900. Inspecting shade-grown tobacco wrapper leaves. Viñales Valley in Pinar del Río, one of Cuba's most spectacular natural wonders and the best tobacco-growing region on earth.

Havana cigars. Part of this strategy was to focus on the product's entirely handmade aspect: growing, harvesting, curing, stripping, blending, rolling, sorting, and packing. In addition, handsome cigar-box artwork—versus the cheap packaging of cigarettes—bespoke quality and tradition. Despite the tyranny of the ubiquitous cigarette, the most famous of the old Cuban brands have survived on the island, including Montecristo, Partagas, Punch, H. Upmann, Romeo y Julieta, and Hoyo de Monterrey.

CLOCKWISE FROM UPPER LEFT: This beautiful cigar-box artwork bespoke quality and tradition. Stripping and sorting tobacco. Promoting Havana cigars at the 1939 New York World's Fair. Cuba's National Commission for Propaganda and Defense of Havana Tobacco suggested visiting Macy's Havana Humidor while in New York. "Look for the green Warranty Stamp of the Cuban Government."

FACING: The Partagas cigar factory in 2007, an obligatory stop while in Havana and home to Cuba's most sophisticated cigar shop.

Havana between the World Wars

"Well-named, the 'Isle of Enchantment' lures the Northern visitor. When icy gales are pounding Boston and New York, while Chicago is blizzard-bound and Winter is king, then Havana, gayest of capitals in the Western Hemisphere, with the balmiest of climates, makes her strongest appeal."

— "Cuba, The Summerland of the World" booklet published by the Winter in Cuba Committee, circa 1921

RIGHT:
During the 1920s and 1930s, Cuba was the playground of America's elite.

With the armistice of World War I, the enactment of Prohibition, and the dawn of the Roaring Twenties, Cuba beckoned. Having been primed with prewar hotels, a national casino, a country club, and the Oriental Park Thoroughbred racetrack, the island was ready to welcome North Americans back to its shores. While Miami had its advantages—sun, luxurious hotels, and ocean breezes—Havana had all that plus liquor, roulette, jai alai, rumba, a seductive nightlife, and the romance of a foreign land. Only ninety miles from Key West via the Peninsular and Occidental Steamship (P&O) Company's SS *Florida*, Havana's attractions also included golf, tennis, polo, sailing, deep-sea fishing, and motoring its scenic byways. Concluded the Winter in Cuba Committee's promotional booklet, "Beauty reigns, relaxation prevails, and by

Havana in the 1920s

THIS PAGE: A short overnight journey via steamship brought American tourists to an exotic foreign land of rum, rumba, and roulette.

FACING, CLOCKWISE FROM UPPER LEFT: 1920s sophisticates celebrate their escape from Prohibition. Three American swells and their Cuban lady friends at the Paddock Bar in the 1930s. Savoring a legal brewski at Havana's Tropical Gardens in 1930. Greeting the SS *Florida*'s arrival in 1940.

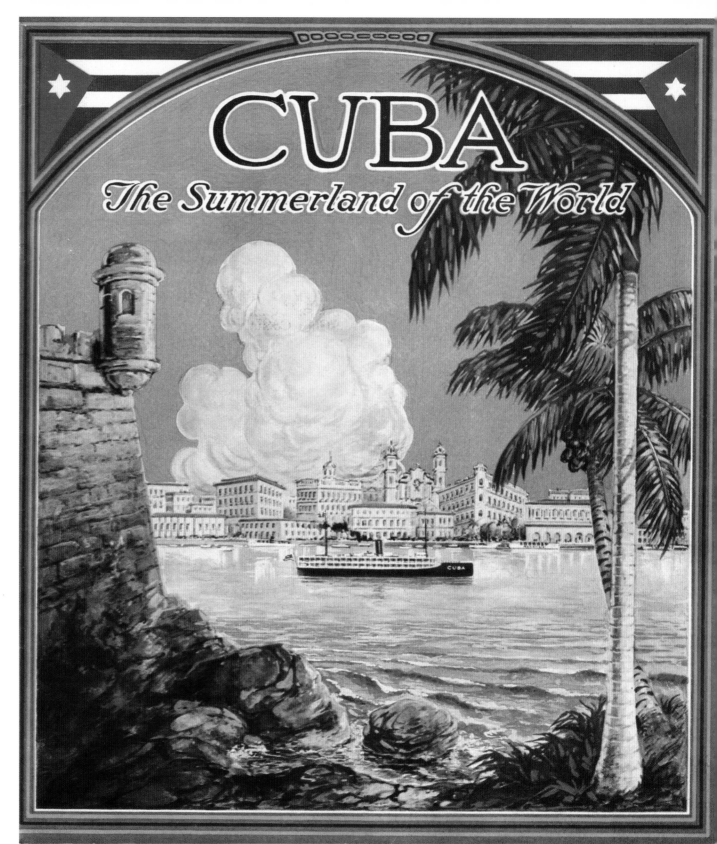

Geyers-Garden-Restaurant
KILOMETRO 16 · ARROYO ARENAS

Manager-Rufino Fernandez
HABANA, CUBA

Shortest Sea Route to Cuba
THE PENINSULAR and OCCIDENTAL STEAMSHIP CO.

Menu

JOCKEY CLUB, HAVANA, CUBA

HABANA. - Carreras de Caballos. Hipódromo Oriental
Oriental Park. - Horse Races Stand

Sevilla-Biltmore   *Habana, Cuba*

courtesy of license your personal liberty is unrestricted. Havana is one of the best-ordered capitals in the world and surely the liveliest."

Into this atmosphere came New York's John McEntee Bowman in 1919, owner of the prestigious Biltmore hotel chain, who immediately purchased and upgraded Havana's venerable Sevilla Hotel, reopening it in grand style as the Sevilla-Biltmore in 1920. With its central location on the Prado, a festive atmosphere, and the addition of a new ten-story tower in 1922, the Sevilla-Biltmore was the most glamorous hostelry in Cuba prior to the construction of the Hotel Nacional in 1930. Guests swooned over the Sevilla-Biltmore's romantic roof garden, which offered spectacular views of the city, Morro Castle, and the Spanish Main with the background of Cuban music drifting up from the hotel's open-air patio below.

Bowman's evident success led to his takeover and management of Havana's Jockey Club, the Oriental Park Racetrack, and the Gran Casino Nacional (which he quickly remodeled), places where both American and Cuban elite gathered to publicly socialize in luxurious style. Of the privileged Habaneros (Havana's local residents), the Winter Committee's booklet noted, "The Cubans, gentry all, who vie with the Americans in their enjoyment of recreation at these famous resorts, are given to large family parties, a sight that always appeals to the American visitors."

John McEntee Bowman

By the mid-1920s, Bowman, an unflagging entrepreneur, had formed the Cuban–American Realty Company, a powerful real estate investment syndicate composed of influential Cuban officials and U.S. financiers whose goal was to exploit Cuba's newfound status as a playground of the rich. Comparing Havana to France's Deauville and Riviera, the company sponsored luxury junkets of America's pleasure-seeking privileged class to experience for themselves the excitement of Cuba. Havana enjoyed an even larger tourist surge following the devastating hurricane of 1926 that laid waste to Miami and its new hotels. Not to be deterred by misfortune, America's winter crowd turned its eyes to a nearby land of sunshine that welcomed them with its amenities intact—Cuba.

In 1928, Bowman's real estate syndicate inaugurated the oceanfront Havana Biltmore Yacht and Country Club, which complemented the prestigious Havana Country Club with its oversubscribed membership in Marianao. Bowman used his new country club as the showplace gateway to the company's adjacent 2,000-acre Biltmore tract, where luxurious vacation homes were anticipated. These would be comparable to the large Spanish- and neoclassical-style winter retreats being built on sprawling estates in Havana's Playa, Miramar, Country Club Park, and Marianao districts for some of America's most prominent industrialists of the 1920s. One of these, chemicals magnate Irénée DuPont, constructed a palatial retreat along

Habana: Edificios Y Campo de Golf en el Country Club
Golfing at Country Club Links.

106247

THIS PAGE: New yacht and country clubs attracted increasing numbers of wealthy Americans to Cuba throughout the 1920s, especially after the 1926 hurricane wrecked Miami's resorts but left Havana unscathed.

FACING: American chemicals tycoon Irénée DuPont built his seaside "Xanadu" residence on unspoiled Varadero Beach in 1927.

HABANA BILTMORE YACHT AND COUNTRY CLUB, HAVANA, CUBA

the then-isolated tropical Varadero Beach, located twenty miles east of Havana, in 1927. DuPont named his estate "Xanadu."

Country club teas and executive banquets might be followed by late-night excursions to the Sans Souci Cabaret and Nightclub, where couples danced under the stars to a mix of popular Cuban and North American tunes played by top orchestras. For upscale gaming, the Gran Casino Nacional beckoned, its risqué fountain nymphs symbolizing Havana's hedonistic gaiety for those able to afford its pleasures.

For the budget tourist—those intent primarily on reaching the nearest tavern upon disembarking the SS *Florida*—there was the Dos Hermanos Bar, conveniently situated across from the passenger piers in Old Havana. Another watering hole popular with Americans was the U.S. Bar (later renamed Ballyhoo), which was located closer to the Prado promenade near the big hotels. But it was the always-packed Sloppy Joe's, adjacent to Ballyhoo, that became the most famous of Havana's many saloons from its

FACING:
Dancing nymphs welcomed guests to the remodeled Gran Casino Nacional. The chic Sans Souci nightclub remained a top attraction from the 1930s until the revolution.

CLOCKWISE FROM ABOVE:
Disembarking Americans make a mad dash to Havana's U.S. Bar during Prohibition. The U.S. Bar's floating welcome wagon. The dockside Dos Hermanos bar/restaurant has operated continuously for over a hundred years.

inception in the 1920s under the ownership of José "Sloppy Joe" Abeal until its demise under Castro. Located in a vast neocolonial building on a busy corner one block from the Sevilla-Biltmore, Sloppy Joe's original Prohibition-era slogan was "First port of call, out where the wet begins."

Havana's accommodations for the increasing waves of American tourists arriving monthly by steamer, and increasingly by airplane, included the hotels Inglaterra, Pasaje, Ambos Mundos, Royal Palm, Bristol, Ritz, Parkview, Presidente, and many others. Among these was the venerable Hotel Plaza with its atmospheric arcade that would appear in the 1959 political satire *Our Man in Havana,* and its casino that was looted on New Year's Day 1959 by celebratory mobs upon learning of Batista's late-night escape.

However, it was the stock market crash of 1929 and the subsequent Great Depression, in addition to the repeal of Prohibition in 1932, that let much of the overheated air out of Cuba's tourism balloon. Yet the dying embers of the Roaring Twenties flared one last time

JOSE ABEAL Y OTERO
"Sloppy Joe"

Sloppy Joe's Bar

José Abeal y Otero (left) had been the proprietor of the most popular bar for Americans in Cuba since the early 1920s. Packed with tourists day and night, Sloppy Joe's not only served cocktails but also sold cigars, sandwiches, and Joe's own brand of bottled rum. To commemorate their visit, tourists often posed for remarkably high-quality souvenir photographs that were mounted on heavy cardboard. Thousands of these pictures still lie hidden in moldy attics and dusty albums across the United States. The bar was best captured in the 1959 film *Our Man in Havana.*

SLOPPY JOE'S BAR
HAVANE

HABANA. Hotel Plaza. Plaza Hotel.

Havana's Finest Hotels

CLOCKWISE FROM FAR LEFT:
The Hotel Plaza has been a Havana institution since 1895, when this postcard was produced. Alec Guinness and Maureen O'Hara in a scene from *Our Man in Havana,* with an atmospheric Hotel Plaza in the background. The Hotel Royal Palm was a top-rated hostelry in the 1920s. The Hotel Plaza in 2007.

with the opening in 1930 of the spectacular Hotel Nacional de Cuba along the Malecón overlooking the sea. Intending the hotel to be the crown jewel of Cuba's tourist industry, President Machado awarded the $4 million commission to the renowned New York architectural firm of McKim, Mead and White in 1928. Begun before the crash and taking two years to construct, the five-hundred-room hotel elegantly blended Spanish, Moorish, classical, and Art Deco elements in its design. Wrote historian Rosalie Schwartz of the project, "The Hotel Nacional was a fitting monument to the president's surging self-importance, fed by bankers

HABANA, PARQUE DEL MAINE — HOTEL NACIONAL

NATIONAL HOTEL — MAINE MEMORIAL

3A-H237

ARTISTAS EN EL HOTEL NACIONAL DE CUBA

ENTERTAINERS AT THE HOTEL NACIONAL DE CUBA

Just in time for the Depression, the Nacional immediately became the country's leading hotel and remained so until the Capri, Riviera, and Hilton hotels opened in the late 1950s. With its prominent seaside location fronting the Malecón in Vedado, the Hotel Nacional de Cuba has hosted presidents, industrialists, film stars, and royalty. It was the crowning achievement of Cuban dictator Gerardo Machado (inset with glasses), seen here with American ambassador Harry Guggenheim in 1931.

HOTEL NACIONAL DE CUBA

PISCINA PRIVADA DE AGUA SALADA. HOTEL NACIONAL DE CUBA

PRIVATE SALT-WATER POOL. HOTEL NACIONAL DE CUBA

LOGGIA DEL HOTEL NACIONAL DE CUBA

IZANDO LA BANDERA EN EL HOTEL NACIONAL DE CUBA

RAISING THE COLORS AT HOTEL NACIONAL DE CUBA

LOGGIA OF THE HOTEL NACIONAL DE CUBA

Despite remodelings by Meyer Lansky in the 1950s and more recently by European investors, the Hotel Nacional has managed to retain its character as the doyenne of Cuban hostelries into the twenty-first century. The photo above depicts the Nacional as it appeared in 2007.

The Tragedy of Cuban Politics

During the fifty-six years of the Cuban Republic, the island was cursed with a succession of presidents of varying degrees of competence and corruption, from the hapless Tomás Estrada Palma to the venal Fulgencio Batista. Although visitors paid scant attention to Cuba's political scene, Cuban politicians utilized their offices to encourage mass tourism—while alternately ignoring or encouraging its vices—as a means of enriching themselves and their cronies.

Amazingly, as the country lurched from one political crisis to the next, there were long periods of actual economic prosperity as Cuba increased its exports of sugar, tobacco, coffee, rum, nickel, and other commodities. However, Cuba's Achilles' heel was an

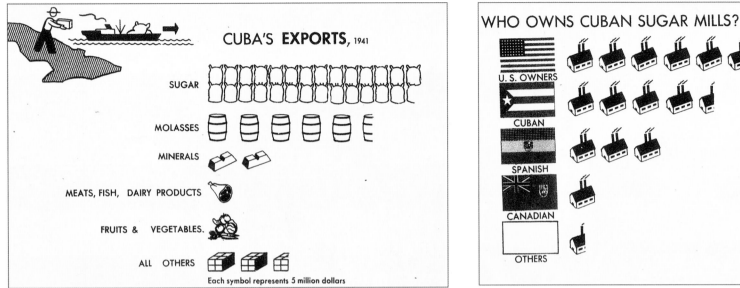

CUBA'S **EXPORTS**, 1941

SUGAR
MOLASSES
MINERALS
MEATS, FISH, DAIRY PRODUCTS
FRUITS & VEGETABLES.
ALL OTHERS

Each symbol represents 5 million dollars

WHO OWNS CUBAN SUGAR MILLS?

U.S. OWNERS
CUBAN
SPANISH
CANADIAN
OTHERS

Each symbol represents 5% of 1939 production

economy dominated by American companies, such as United Fruit, and a relatively small Cuban elite. This was particularly evident in the contrast between prosperous Havana and the country's desperately poor rural areas, where the growing seeds of discontent would be harvested by Castro and his revolution.

Only four years after Governor General Leonard Wood officially relinquished America's sovereignty to President Estrada Palma, American soldiers once again marched in to quell the fraternal warfare that had erupted between the young nation's major political parties. Following another two years of American rule, a new president, José Miguel Gomez, was elected in 1908 and assumed office. Gregarious and dishonest in equal measure, Gomez (1908–1912) was followed by the more subdued but equally crooked Mario García Menocal (1912–1920), who commissioned the grand presidential palace soon occupied by incoming president Alfredo Zayas

(1920–1924). As with his predecessors, Zayas's four years in office provided ample time for he and his cronies to succeed in enriching themselves via an astounding assortment of embezzlement schemes involving unbuilt bridges, roads, and civic buildings.

But the Gomez/Menocal/Zayas troika was no match for the level of unrestrained wealth and power accumulated by the former cattle rustler Gerardo Machado, who served as president from 1924 until he outraced the motorcar posse of gun-firing revolutionaries that chased his departing airplane as he fled into exile in 1933.

Not surprisingly, given the length of his rule and his ability to siphon construction

ABOVE:
Sugar dominated Cuba's economy, with the majority of the industry controlled by American companies.

BELOW:
The flamboyant new presidential palace was completed in 1921.

HABANA:—NUEVO PALACIO PRESIDENCIAL

NEW PRESIDENT'S PALACE.

El Presidente

The El Presidente was a popular cocktail in Havana during Prohibition, when legions of alcohol-deprived Americans descended on the city by air and sea; it was named in honor of Mario García Menocal, president of Cuba from 1912 to 1920. Recipes varied widely; this one hails from the 1955 guide *What, When, Where And How To Drink*, by Richard L. Williams and David Myers.

—Jeff Berry

El Presidente

1 1/2 ounces aged gold rum
1/2 ounce orange curaçao
1/2 ounce dry white vermouth
Dash grenadine

Stir everything with ice until well chilled. Strain into a cocktail glass. Garnish with a twist of orange peel.

ABOVE:
President Machado (center) directs his officers to quell an uprising in Santa Clara in 1931.

funds, Gerardo Machado's dictatorship led to the building of prominent public works that would prove popular with wealthy Cubanos and American tourists in the coming decades. The Capitolio (capitol building), Cuba's central highway, the national library, the national museum, and the wide, landscaped Fifth Avenue that ran through upscale Miramar are examples. Similarly, the latter years of Fulgencio Batista's dictatorship in the 1950s saw the erection of Havana's modern civic center, transit tunnels, airport expansion, and large-scale hotels.

Throughout these years the United States meddled in Cuban affairs to a greater or lesser degree, depending on the vagaries of U.S. politics or the cunning of Cuba's officials at confounding the resident American ambassador at the time. There is no doubt, however, that the American government supported Cuba's corrupt and repressive regimes as bulwarks against meaningful political, economic, or social reform—anything that would interfere with American business interests in the country. Photographs of Cuban officials such as Machado and Batista socializing with American presidents reinforced these bonds.

With the fall of Machado came the meteoric rise of Fulgencio Batista, who would dominate Cuban politics for the next quarter century. Taking advantage of the chaos following Machado's August 1933 escape, Fulgencio Batista Zaldívar, an obscure, handsome, and charismatic sergeant stenographer from Cuba's rural east, mobilized his fellow sergeants at the army's Camp Columbia to defy the officer corps and join with Havana University's revolutionary student movement in overthrowing the unstable interim government. This "Sergeants' Revolution" quickly installed a fiery populist professor and physician—Dr. Ramón Grau San Martín—as provisional president to satisfy the demands of the students, whose leaders included Eduardo Chibás and Carlos Prío Socarrás, two men who would later have a profound influence on the country's destiny. However, President Grau's pro-labor policies and anti-American stance led to his ouster by Batista after only four months in office.

Following Grau, a parade of five puppet presidents left scarcely a trace during the chaotic years of the Great Depression. Unabashedly wearing the mantle of the country's savior, Batista celebrated the fifth anniversary of his glorious coup by presiding over an all-day ceremony in 1938 featuring invitations bearing his likeness chiseling the great statue of the Cuban Republic. Also that year, Batista retained the services of American gangster and renowned gambler Meyer Lansky, who was invited to the island to

professionalize Cuba's Gran Casino Nacional, which had been tainted by a reputation of rigged table games that was keeping America's high rollers away. It was a mutually beneficial relationship that would prove long lasting and especially fruitful during Batista's second administration fifteen years later.

quickly left the island for Daytona Beach, Florida. Following a tumultuous public welcome, the hapless Grau allowed rampant corruption to quickly taint his administration to an extent that soon mirrored Cuba's kleptocracies of the 1910s and 1920s.

Disillusioned by Grau and disgusted by blatant graft, Chibás took his grievances to the airwaves in impassioned and highly popular weekly radio broadcasts that denounced by name those corrupt officials against whom he had gathered incriminating evidence. In 1947, in announcing his candidacy for president, Chibás broke from Grau's tainted Auténticos and formed the Cuban Peoples' Party, known as the Ortodoxos (orthodox Auténticos). Chibás's presidential platform was predicated on bringing honesty to government—his slogan was "Verguenza contra Dinero" ("Honor versus Money").

¡VERGÜENZA contra DINERO!

¡LIBERTAD ¿ MUERTE!

Although losing the 1948 presidential election to former comrade and Auténticos candidate Carlos Prío Socarrás, Chibás came in a strong second, setting himself up as the top contender for the job in 1952. Meanwhile, former president Batista, who had been living in exile in Florida, was elected senator *in absentia* in 1948 on the Liberal–Democratic ticket.

The dashingly handsome Prío's reputation had been built many years earlier when, as a student agitator, he helped lead the fight against the Machado dictatorship. For this he spent three years in prison. By 1948, however, the forty-five-year-old Prío had evolved into a wily politician whose management style as president led to an administration as rife with sleaze as his predecessor Grau's. Once again,

FACING:
Batista chisels Cuba's Statue of the Republic in honor of the fifth anniversary of his "Sergeants' Revolution."

ABOVE:
Hapless president Grau and the First Lady in 1947.

RIGHT:
The martyred Eduardo Chibás (left) and 26-year-old Fidel Castro appear on an Ortodoxos campaign poster under the slogans "Honor versus Money!" and "Liberty or Death!" in 1952.

The 1940 presidential election pitted Batista against the one-time provisional president Dr. Grau San Martín. With Batista's win came the passage of the remarkably progressive constitution of 1940 that, had it been respected by future Cuban governments, might have saved the republic from impending upheavals.

While out of power, perpetual presidential candidate Grau had formed the Cuban Revolutionary Party, known as the Auténticos, under the slogan "Cuba for the Cubans." With strong support from the former student radicals of 1933, Eduardo Chibás and Carlos Prío Socarrás, Dr. Grau succeeded in routing Batista's handpicked candidate in 1944. A chastened Batista

Eduardo Chibás used his Sunday radio addresses to denounce government corruption in broadcasts that became increasingly hysterical and vitriolic. On August 5, 1951, Chibás concluded a particularly venomous broadcast chastened by his inability to produce the irrefutable evidence of graft by the minister of education that he had promised listeners the previous week. In a bizarre crescendo to this diatribe, the distraught Chibás pulled out a pistol and shot himself in the stomach, dying from his wounds a week later. Of the thousands of crestfallen mourners who attended Chibás's funeral was the twenty-five-year-old

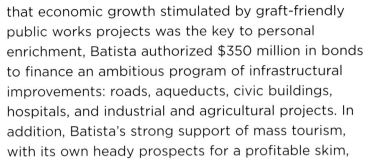

lawyer Fidel Castro, a passionate Chibás acolyte who would compete in the June 1952 election as a candidate of Chibás's Ortodoxos party for the Cuban House of Representatives.

But Senator Fulgencio Batista had other ideas. Recognizing that he was last in the polls for the upcoming presidential election in which he was a candidate, on March 10, 1952, Batista marched into the army's Camp Columbia and declared the Prío government illegitimate, canceling the June elections and, "to save the country from chaotic conditions," moved into the presidential palace without firing a shot. Prío and his family sought refuge in the Mexican embassy, leaving by airplane a few days later.

Following the failure of the courts to dislodge Batista, an outraged Castro organized a small rebel force of 165 men to attack the army's Moncada barracks in Santiago de Cuba as the first strike of yet another Cuban revolutionary movement. On July 26, 1953, Castro's quixotic attempt to storm the fortified barracks ended in the death of seventy of his men and the capture of the remainder, including Fidel and his brother Raul. The sensational trial of Castro and his followers concluded with the revolutionary leader defiantly boasting "La historia me absolvera" ("History will absolve me") as he was sentenced to fifteen years in prison on Cuba's Isle of Pines.

President Batista, meanwhile, set about to establish a dictatorship the likes of which Cuba had not seen since the days of Gerardo Machado. Recognizing

that economic growth stimulated by graft-friendly public works projects was the key to personal enrichment, Batista authorized $350 million in bonds to finance an ambitious program of infrastructural improvements: roads, aqueducts, civic buildings, hospitals, and industrial and agricultural projects. In addition, Batista's strong support of mass tourism, with its own heady prospects for a profitable skim, led to the passage in 1955 of tax breaks and subsidies that immediately resulted in a mad rush of investment by American interests—from the likes of Meyer Lansky and Santo Trafficante to Conrad Hilton—to make Havana the Las Vegas of the Caribbean.

Anxious to remove the stigma of having seized office via a coup, Batista sought to legitimize his rule by staging an election for November 1954. Running as the candidate of his Progressive Action Party (PAP), Batista's only challenger was the former president and now-septuagenarian Grau San Martín. Grau, however, withdrew prior to the polling to protest a blatantly rigged election. Nonetheless, the newly "elected" president Batista felt secure enough in his position to magnanimously offer a general amnesty to political prisoners, including Fidel and Raúl Castro, who immediately left for Mexico to plot Batista's overthrow under the banner of the Twenty-Sixth of July Movement (M-26-7), the date of the Moncada barracks attack. Castro returned at the end of 1956 aboard the American yacht *Granma* that was overloaded with eighty-one revolutionaries, Che Guevara among them. Swept off course by turbulent surf, the *Granma* ran aground along the treacherous coast of Cuba's Oriente province. While Castro's force slogged through murky swamps, a coast guard vessel spotted the *Granma* and soon the government's forces had tracked down and killed all but Fidel, Raul, Che, and nine others. With the help of local *campesinos*, the remnant invaders escaped into the rugged Sierra Maestra to form the core of a revolutionary force that, in two years, would vanquish an army of thirty thousand men.

New York Times Havana correspondent Ruby Hart Phillips reported of Castro's *Granma* adventure in 1956:

> Commerce and industry were prospering, the tourist season was good, the government was pouring millions in public works and new industry. Capital hoped that the government would crush the tiny rebellion without loss of time. Only the youth of the island was solidly behind Fidel Castro with his avowed intention of overthrowing the Batista regime. Only boys and girls from 12 to 25 believed it could be done, and they went into action. Terrorism flared. Bombs exploded; trains were derailed; towns were blacked out by sabotage of power lines; incendiary fires were started by the young revolutionists.

In maintaining his power, Batista resorted to increasingly repressive methods, establishing the much-feared Servicio de Inteligencia Militar or SIM (secret police), whose task it was to root out, torture, and often kill anyone perceived to be a threat to the regime. As Batista grew more desperate, the political

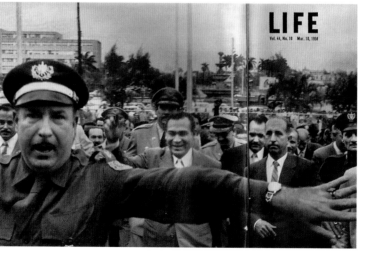

ABOVE:
Batista's army.

LEFT:
Making way for Batista in 1958.

FACING, LEFT:
Castro's army.

FACING, RIGHT:
The rebels disembark from the overloaded *Granma* into treacherous swamps.

murders increased such that by 1958, public revulsion toward the government was widespread among all levels of society. By the end of the year the U.S. government itself had cut off arms shipments to the regime as the eastern provinces were falling to rebel forces, tourism was beginning to decline, and Batista was secretly burning documents in preparation for a New Year's Eve surprise.

Yet, for American tourists and the average Habanero, the 1950s would also be remembered as a culturally rich and exceptionally vibrant time in Havana. If not for Batista's blatant mockery of the democratic process, his close ties to American gambling interests, his transparent corruption, and his brutal suppression of dissent, it is probable that Cuba would have avoided the convulsive transformation of Castro's revolution—for all of its achievements and failures—and the resulting tragedy of the Cuban diaspora.

CUBA 2¢

EL DESEMBARCO DEL "GRANMA"

Cuba's Postwar Tourist Explosion

"Cuba—So Near . . . And Yet So Foreign"
—Slogan, Cuban Tourist Commission, 1940s–1950s

ABOVE RIGHT:
All aboard Cubana Airlines' sleek
Constellation aircraft to Havana.

RIGHT:
Varadero Beach, a "Rhapsody in Blue."

It was close, it was inexpensive, and the tourist police spoke English: after World War II Cuba became the primary exotic destination for Americans who were finally ready to dip their toes into foreign waters without having to venture too far from familiar shores.

The business of mass tourism was a product of the post–World War II period when average Americans, freed of the Great Depression's deprivations, were finally able to embrace

VARADERO

LEFT: Welcome to Cuba, indeed!

ABOVE: The hit song "The Peanut Vendor" introduced Cuban music to Americans in the early 1930s.

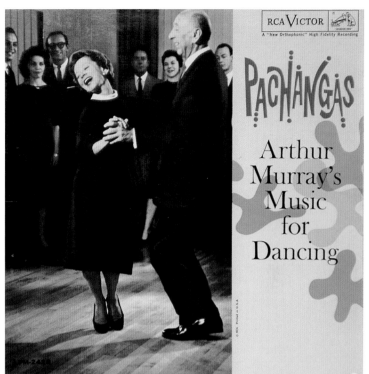

the concept of leisure time. In contrast with the 1920s and 1930s, when tourists to Cuba were generally of the wealthier class, suddenly the island was within the reach of ordinary Americans with disposable incomes and a week or two of vacation time.

Cuba was not completely foreign to most Americans, due to the pervasive influence of the island's intoxicating music played by dance orchestras at that time. The rumba (or rhumba) had been popular since the early 1930s when the song "The Peanut Vendor" from the film *The Cuban Love Song* became a hit, introducing Afro-Cuban percussion instruments and rhythms to the United States. After World War II, the rumba dance craze was followed by mambomania when Cuban Pérez Prado brought the mambo to American audiences via live performances and his many records.

From the mambo emerged the cha-cha-chá, with dance steps made easy by Arthur Murray at his famous dance studios around the country. Because of the enormous popularity of Cuban music and Latin dancing in the States, it was natural that Americans would want to visit the land of the music's origin.

Other popular cultural influences included America's musical theatre. *Guys and Dolls,* the smash Broadway musical that opened in 1950, had as its central storyline a wager by gambler Sky Masterson that he could convince the shy, introverted Sarah Brown to join him for a weekend jaunt in naughty Havana. Masterson wins the bet, and the reserved Sarah finds in Havana the joys of life that she had thus far shunned—romance and music, dance and laughter under tropical stars. For uptight

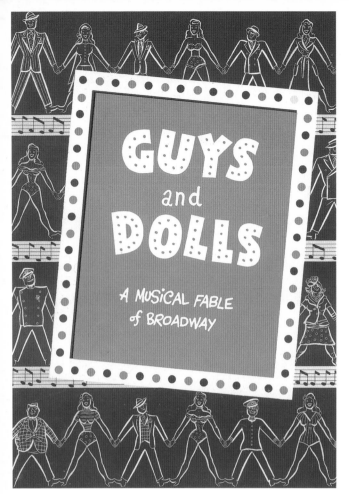

1950s America, the tale was a heady invitation to experience Cuba for itself.

Meanwhile, the real-life romance of Lucille Ball and her handsome Cuban singer/bandleader husband Desi Arnaz, as depicted on the top-rated *I Love Lucy* television show that premiered in 1951, made Americans feel more comfortable with Cubans and their culture. Prior to television, Desi Arnaz had become famous for making the Cuban song "Babalu" a popular hit and his theme song. He also starred in the rumba movie musicals *Cuban Pete* in 1946 and *Holiday in Havana* in 1949. Desi's films were just a few of the many musical comedies that Hollywood had been producing since the 1930s that glamorized a Havana of tropical romance, dazzling outdoor nightclubs, and swank casinos.

Getting to Cuba became easier after the war as transportation options to the "Tropical Holiday Isle" were more numerous than in the 1930s, and air travel was no longer perceived as such an extravagance. A Pan American Airways 1947 brochure intoned, "Carefree Cuba, Pearl of the Antilles, is calling you to share her enticing charms.

Sexy singer-bandleader

Desi Arnaz personified modern Cuba, reassuring skittish Americans that Cuba wasn't really too foreign after all.

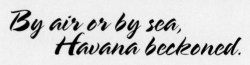

By air or by sea,
Havana beckoned.

HAVANA

AIR *and* SEA CRUISES *from* MIAMI

VIA PAN AMERICAN WORLD AIRWAYS
CUBANA AIRWAYS • NATIONAL AIRLINES
S/S FLORIDA

SIGHTSEEING
with
Manuel Valdes

There's no better way to join the fun than by Flying Clipper. From Miami, take your choice of many flights every day and in mere minutes you're in a 'foreign' land—Cuba, so friendly, so gay, so exciting, you'll want to stay—forever."

In addition, the air fleets of Braniff, National, and Delta offered many travel options to Havana and the Caribbean. The sleek Constellation aircraft of Cubana Airlines not only covered routes from New York and Miami to twenty cities in Cuba but also served Lisbon and Madrid. Not to be ignored, the P&O Steamship Company's reliable SS *Florida* continued to ply the waters between Miami and Havana Harbor—where taking your own car to Cuba via

FAR LEFT:
The P&O steamship line encouraged Americans to explore Cuba in their own cars.

LEFT, ABOVE, AND FACING:
Sightseeing tours and gala nightclub excursions kept the tourists busy.

steamship or ferry became a popular way of exploring the island on familiar tires.

A brilliant response to the travel insecurities of Americans was the marketing of low-cost package tours to Cuba. It became obvious that most Americans were more comfortable joining a group of like-minded tourists where all the myriad details of travel were pre-planned on precise timetables. On a group tour all one had to do was show up and be whisked away from one "must see" destination to the next.

Once in Cuba, those with more open schedules could choose from a host of local tour companies offering half-day and full-day sightseeing trips to the city's major attractions, as well as night excursions to popular bars, cabarets, casinos, and nightclubs.

A brochure for "Sightseeing with Manuel Valdes" offered the exhausting three-hour "City Circle Tour," a twenty-five-mile exploration of "entertainment and educational opportunities," including the following:

Government Buildings: Presidential Palace, the National Capitol, Havana City Hall, Police Castle Headquarters, Principe Penitentiary, Orphanage and Department of State.

Points of Historical Interest: Mercy Church, El Templete, La Fuerza Fort, Plaza de Armas Square, La Punta Castle, Student's Monument, Maine Memorial, Maximo Gomez and Maceo Monuments, ruins of old Havana City Wall, complete coverage of streets of old Colonial Havana and the actual spots where former political revolts and buccaneer raids took place.

Medical Cooperatives: Centro Asturiano, Gallego and the Dependientes.

Parks: Maceo, Marti, Central Park Botanical Gardens, Prado or Paseo de Marti and other smaller parks.

Working Class Districts: Jesus Maria tenements, a hobo town and some slum areas.

Aristocratic Residential Districts: Vedado, Malecon and surrounding areas.

Shopping Centers: The department store section of Galiano, San Rafael and the Prado, side street curio shops, and the Havana Garment Center.

Cigar Factory: A stop will be made at the well-known 'La Corona-Cabanas' cigar factory and Tobacco Museum. Here you will be shown the process of rolling the 'La Corona-Cabanas' cigars recognized as the world's finest.

Miscellaneous: Columbus Cemetery and Trocadero Rum Distillery.

"After this trip is over," the brochure concluded, "unlike others that are not systematically planned, you will know Havana. We make the distillery the last stop where you will get free drinks and you will have frozen daiquiris to your heart's content."

Indeed, a pitcher of daiquiris would only begin to soothe a throbbing headache from experiencing in three hours what should have taken three days to explore.

Similarly, Embajada Tours offered the whirlwind "A Gala Night in Havana" with "Three Fabulous

King Salomon's Store. Open day and night - **Prado 515**

Shows all in One Night." For $10.75 you would be whisked from one cabaret show to another, visiting the Sans Souci, Tropicana, and Bambu nightclubs, arriving back at your hotel in the wee small hours of the morning.

For your shopping pleasure, King Salomon's Store on the Prado specialized in cigars, liquors, perfumes, and alligator goods promoted in a brochure that also included a Spanish–English guide with such helpful phrases as:

Take us to King Salomon's Store.
　—*Queremos que nos lleve a King Salomon's.*

We want to have a good time.
　—*Queremos pasar un rato divertido.*

Give me a kiss.
—*Deme un beso.*

I want to buy a good cigar.
—*Quiero comprar un buen tabaco.*

We want to go to the casino.
—*Queremos ir al casino.*

You are very charming.
—*Es usted muy simpatico.*

And Bacardi made it easy to bring home bottles of its assorted rums with handy cardboard carry-on boxes available in local shops.

Varadero Beach, the strip of sand on which chemical industry tycoon Irénée DuPont had built his Xanadu in the 1920s had, by the 1950s, become one of the Caribbean's top beach resorts. Popular with American sunbathers, deep-sea fishermen, and rich Habaneros eager to escape the city, Varadero welcomed them all with accommodations ranging from modest bungalows to lavish hotels such as William Liebow's Late Moderne–style Hotel Varadero Internacional, erected in 1950. In addition, Varadero sprouted a row of millionaire's mansions, including one of President Batista's sprawling retreats.

Following his takeover of the government in 1952, Batista actively encouraged tourism as both a means of diversifying the country's agricultural-based economy and enriching himself and his cronies. In 1953, to counter bad publicity surrounding crooked games at local casinos, Batista put mobster Meyer Lansky back on the government payroll as gambling supervisor in charge of cleaning up Havana's games of chance, reassuring tourists that Cuba's casinos were as honest as those in Las Vegas. In fact, Vegas, America's Sin City, was indeed the premier gambling

FACING:
From brandy to alligator handbags, King Salomon's had it all.

RIGHT:
Washed ashore with her maracas on Varadero Beach.

FAR RIGHT:
Enjoying a sunny serenade or reeling in a big one: Varadero was Cuba's top beach resort.

and entertainment mecca that Batista yearned to emulate in Havana. To that end, Batista enacted Hotel Law 2074 in 1955, which provided the tax breaks, government loans, and other incentives for Lansky, his crime-syndicate colleagues, and even American corporations to invest in building the extravagant hotel-casinos that are perhaps the most potent image of Havana prior to Castro's revolution—a period that lasted less than three years.

And it was not just the big boys who found Havana an alluring investment opportunity in the 1950s. The number of the city's bars, restaurants, cabarets, nightclubs, shops, and midsized hotels increased in line with the tourist boom to the benefit of many Habaneros.

Yet, as important as Las Vegas was in influencing Havana's growth, it was Miami Beach that was the main competition to Havana's charms. Since World War II, the balmy south Florida resort had experienced spectacular growth far exceeding Cuba's capital city. Situated only 220 miles north of Havana, Miami Beach had Cuba's weather, sunny beaches, and, most importantly, the security of being in the United States of America. Hotels like the Eden Roc, Saxony, Fontainebleau, Nautilus, and Shelborne were

View of Hotel Internacional, from Main Entrance, Veradero Beach, Cuba

more modern and luxurious than any of Havana's hotels with the exception of the Capri, Riviera, and Hilton that opened after 1956. Regardless, Cuba's Tourist Commission boasted of Havana in 1957:

Here is a new world, a gay world—whirling with excitement and beauty—a kaleidoscope of shifting colors and moods! Havana—a city of singing hearts and dancing feet, of smiles and spice and a rumba beat. Here is a fabulous blend of the old and the new—truly Latin America, where ancient Spanish culture meets the modern world. A magic city of vivid contrasts, Havana is big and gay—a place to have wonderful fun!

The fun, however, began to dissipate in 1958 when even the Tourist Commission's propaganda machine couldn't drown out the ever-more-frequent bombings and news of Castro's growing rebellion in the east.

Exciting ... Foreign

CUBA

Where Yesterday Meets Tomorrow

Ancient cathedrals and forts, modern hotels, nightclubs and gaming casinos. Scenic beauty throughout the provinces ... flowers, mountains, the sea and the world's most beautiful beaches.

From New York ... **4½ hours non-stop**
From Miami ... **One Hour by Air**
Overnight by Cruise Ship
... or Drive by Auto Ferry,
Key West to Havana
NO PASSPORT REQUIRED

CUBAN **T**OURIST **C**OMMISSION
610 Fifth Ave., N.Y.   336 E. Flagler, Miami   P.O. Box 1609, Havana

Drinking, Dining, and Dancing

"This is Cuba, Mister."
—Tropicana comedy revue, 1958

cradle of the frozen daiquiri

FLORIDITA

RIGHT:
The dynamic Mary and Rudy dancers "Los Torbellinos del Tropico" ("The Tropical Whirlpool") perform on a popular Havana television show.

As the nightlife capital of the Caribbean, Havana had hundreds of bars, restaurants, and clubs, from seedy dives to fabulous showrooms, all over the city. The most popular nightspots were concentrated near the Prado, central Havana's promenade, or in the vicinity of Calle 23 (Twenty-Third Street), a sloping thoroughfare known as La Rampa in the city's sophisticated Vedado district.

SLOPPY·JOE'S·BAR

HAVANA·CUBA·

PRICE: 50¢ EACH

Among Havana's bars, Sloppy Joe's was in a league all its own, having maintained its reputation as the most popular watering hole for Americans from Prohibition through the Batista years. Havana's Sloppy Joe's existed long before the Key West version of the same name. During the 1930s, Sloppy Joe published small pocket-sized cocktail manuals that included a short history of the bar. According to the booklet, José Abeal, a Spanish emigrant who had worked for many years as a bartender in both New Orleans and Havana, converted a small grocery store on the corner of Obispo and Zulueta streets into a saloon in 1918. While several American friends were visiting José "and seeing the poor appearance and filthy-looking condition of the place, one of them said 'Why, Joe, this place is certainly sloppy, look at the filthy water running from under the counter.' From here on, the name Sloppy Joe stuck to José Abeal as part of his own life and was destined to make him and his business famous and internationally known." Curiously, there were other legends regarding the bar's odd name, including one involving a vindictive

Sloppy Joe's Then and Now

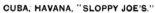

CUBA, HAVANA, "SLOPPY JOE'S."

FACING, LEFT:
Sloppy Joe's circa 1927.

FACING, RIGHT:
The same view in 2007 during its reconstruction. Sloppy Joe's closed after suffering a devastating fire in the 1960s.

Sloppy Joe's

"Sloppy Joe is not Cuba," Sydney Clark scolded readers of his 1946 travel guide, *All The Best In Cuba.* He was bemoaning that most American tourists went straight from their cruise ships to Sloppy Joe's Bar, and then straight back to their ships. Joe's was the only thing they saw in Havana, despite the fact that, according to Clark, the bar served "ordinary drinks in a wholly undistinguished setting." Its patrons were 90 percent American tourists, lured to Joe's by the power of marketing (proprietor José "Sloppy Joe" Abeal had been made into a legendary figure by his journalist regulars) and the comfort of the familiar (Cuban citizens dismissed Joe's as an "American" bar). But after obtaining a Sloppy Joe's recipe booklet dating from the 1935 tourist season, we differ with Sydney Clark on one point: Joe's drinks were anything but ordinary. In fact, most were quite inventive, such as this 1935 signature drink.

—Jeff Berry

Sloppy Joe's

2 ounces pineapple juice
1 ounce cognac
1 ounce port wine
1/4 teaspoon orange curaçao
1/4 teaspoon grenadine

Shake well with plenty of crushed ice. Pour into a tall glass. Serve with a straw.

Havana newspaperman who, having been ejected from the joint by Abeal after refusing to pay his bar tab, retaliated by opining in his column that the bar should be called Sloppy Joe's on account of its dirty appearance.

Having opened just as Prohibition's priggish restrictions were shuttering bars from New York to Los Angeles, Sloppy Joe's welcomed Americans for over four decades with a cocktail menu consisting of over eighty recipes, including the American Girl, Blue Moon, Mary Pickford, Millionaire, Around the World, Miami, Havana, Fox Movietone News [!], and the house drink—Sloppy Joe's. Like most Havana pubs, Sloppy Joe's also sold sandwiches, cigars, and bottled booze. Indeed, Sloppy Joe's bar was stocked to the rafters with display cases containing its own brand of twelve-year-old rum.

After World War II, Sloppy Joe's original

Prohibition-era slogan "First port of call, out where the wet begins" became "Where the great of the world and the not-so-great meet daily." One of the world's greats who dropped by was Frank Sinatra during a visit to Havana in December 1946 in the company of his buddies the Fischetti brothers, Joe and Rocco, gangster cousins of Al Capone. Not coincidentally, Ol' Blue Eyes and the boys were in Cuba for the infamous mafia summit of 1946 held at Havana's Hotel Nacional, where exiled mob boss Lucky Luciano formally anointed Meyer Lansky as Cuba's gambling syndicate boss.

Not far from Sloppy Joe's was the famous La Floridita bar/restaurant, renowned as the "cuna del daiquiri" ("cradle of the daiquiri"). La Floridita was

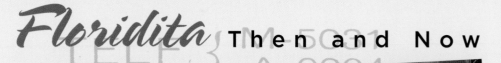

Floridita Then and Now

The Floridita

Remarkably, from the furnishings to the place settings, the Floridita hasn't changed in fifty years, retaining the historic character—and sublime daiquiri cocktails—that Hemingway would recognize if he were alive today.

CLOCKWISE FROM ABOVE:
Floridita dining room circa 1955. The bar circa 1955. The restaurant in 2007.

FACING:
The bar in 2007.

La Floridita Daiquiri

Legend has it that that Jennings Cox, an American engineer working at a Cuban copper mine near the coastal town of Daiquiri, invented the daiquiri cocktail one evening after work in 1896. A conflicting story places the birth of the daiquiri in Santiago de Cuba circa 1898, when a U.S. soldier named William Shafter added ice to a local Cuban drink of rum, lime, and sugar. Whatever its origin, no one disputes that the best daiquiris in Cuba were mixed by Constantino Ribalaigua, who presided over Havana's La Floridita bar from 1912 to 1952. Ernest Hemingway was a big fan of Constantino, who invented the *Papa Dobles* grapefruit daiquiri for him; Trader Vic Bergeron traveled from San Francisco to Havana just to watch Constantino make a daiquiri in person. No wonder La Floridita came to be known as "the cradle of the daiquiri." The German author Charles Schumann unearthed Constantino's recipe in his 1986 *Tropical Bar Book*.

—Jeff Berry

La Floridita Daiquiri

1 ounce fresh lime juice
1/4 ounce sugar syrup
1/4 ounce Maraschino liqueur
13/4 ounces white rum

Shake well with a generous scoop of crushed ice.
Strain into a pre-chilled cocktail glass.

founded by Constantino Ribalaigua, who is credited with perfecting the frozen daiquiri in the 1930s. It was also famous for its fine cuisine served in the elegant surroundings of an ornate dining room that was popular with visitors such as British novelist Graham Greene.

Next door to La Floridita along Calle Montserrate remains Havana's oldest restaurant, La Zaragozana, which was established in 1830 as a Spanish bistro specializing in Galician stew. In 1955, the restaurant celebrated its 125th anniversary by opening "Rincon Aragones," a re-creation of an ancient Spanish tavern

RIGHT:
La Florida founder Constantino Ribalaigua pours a drink for a chic Prohibition-era couple at his famous bar. (Note: the names La Florida and La Floridita refer to the same establishment.)

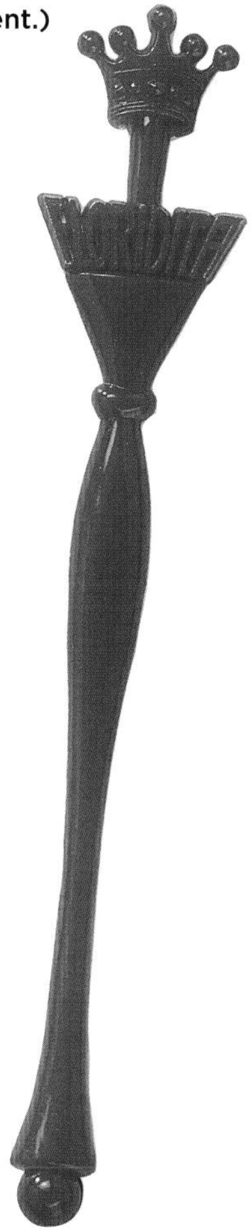

"LA FLORIDA"
BAR Y RESTAURANT

THE GRADLE OF THE DAYQUIRI COCKTAIL

FOTO S. MIGUEL No. 5   MONTSERRAT & OBISPO ST.

ABOVE:
The Spanish La Zaragozana restaurant as depicted in 1955.

RIGHT:
The restaurant in 2007.

ABOVE AND RIGHT:
The Mandarin in Havana's swank Vedado district was "the most luxurious Chinese Restaurant in the Americas," according to its circa-1958 postcard.

FAR RIGHT:
Had enough of rice, beans, and chicken? Try Moishe Pipik. It's strictly kosher.

dining room "decorated with real Spanish antiques and typical paintings where patrons feel as if in a fascinating corner of Old Spain." La Zaragozana, with its 1955 interior still intact, turned 175 in 2005.

In addition to dozens of Cuban, Spanish, and seafood restaurants, Havana also had Willie's Restaurant (American), the Mandarin (Chinese), Frascati (Italian), Restaurant Vienes (Viennese), and Moishe Pipik's Jewish Delicatessen. Topping all

Air conditioned   21 y O, Vedado

Monseigneur

The rendezvous of the Social Elite

A corner of Paris in the great Havana

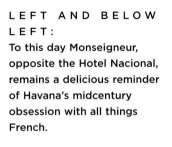

non-Cuban influences, however, was that of France. In 1950s Havana a general rule was, if it's French, it must be classy. The majority of the city's top nighttime venues had French names, many with ornate furnishings to match. These included the big nightclubs—Montmartre, Sans Souci, and the Hotel Nacional's Club Parisienne—and numerous bars and restaurants such as Club Les Amants, El Palacio de Cristal (Crystal Palace), Dan Sima's Atelier Club, La Rue 19, Normandie, and L'aiglon Dining Room at the Havana Riviera. And featured at the air-conditioned Monseigneur (its restaurant open from noon to dawn) was a French violin ensemble "under the direction of Professor Pego"!

For those seeking "bohemian" Havana, there was (and is) La Bodeguita del Medio, a hole-in-the-wall where locals, tourists, and celebrities could safely go slumming. Also known as "La B del M" and located in Old Havana just down the

LEFT AND BELOW LEFT:
To this day Monseigneur, opposite the Hotel Nacional, remains a delicious reminder of Havana's midcentury obsession with all things French.

BELOW RIGHT:
El Palacio de Cristal: "Delightful, exclusive, a corner of Paris in Havana," circa 1957.

EL PALACIO DE CRISTAL
BAR ★ RESTAURANT FRANCES
San José y Consulado   Habana   Telf W 4306   M-4430

street from the venerable Hotel Ambos Mundos (where Ernest Hemingway once resided), the tavern started out in 1942 as Angel Martinez's small general store prior to its transformation into the celebrated down-market pub famous for its mojito cocktails. According to legend, the hard-drinking Hemingway remarked, "I take my mojitos at La Bodeguita and my daiquiris at La Floridita."

In creating La B del M, it took a raffish Hungarian expatriate named Sepy Dobronyi to convince owner Martinez to convert his store into a tavern in 1951. Sepy, a swarthy ex-fighter pilot, jewelry designer, metalworker, photographer, sculptor, painter, and skin diver, was "the dynamic force that [kept] La

LEFT: "La B del M," mojito central, in 2007.

BELOW: It was the raffish Hungarian expatriate Sepy (lower right) who inspired La Bodeguita's bohemian reputation in the 1950s.

Mojito

The mojito is the drink of the moment: It's served in trendy bars and restaurants; it's sold premixed in bottles by big liquor conglomerates; and it's even the star of its own commercial, in which an impossibly handsome bartender muddles a mojito in time to the techno beat of a hip nightclub. One might be forgiven for assuming that the mojito is a new drink, but it first came to fame at La Bodeguita del Medio over fifty years ago. The Havana bar was to the mojito what La Floridita was to the daiquiri. Errol Flynn and Nat King Cole were La Bodeguita fans, as were Fidel Castro and Che Guevara. Fidel's patronage may account for the fact that the bar survived his revolution and is still serving mojitos to busloads of foreign tourists today. The cocktail historian Wayne Curtis, who dubbed La Bodeguita "Havana's mojito mecca" in his 2006 book, *And A Bottle Of Rum: A History Of The New World In Ten Cocktails*, offers the authentic recipe.

—Jeff Berry

Mojito

6 freshly washed mint leaves
2 teaspoons bar sugar
3/4 ounce fresh lime juice
2 ounces good aged rum
Soda water

Muddle the mint, sugar, and lime juice in a tall glass. Add rum. Fill glass with ice. Top with soda. Garnish with mint sprigs.

Bodeguita the center of Cuban bohemia," according to liner notes from a high-fidelity LP that Sepy produced in 1957. The album, recorded in La B del M's back room, featured the tavern's popular musical trio. "Two guitars and maracas, together with three blending voices, provide the very listenable, extremely melodic background for dining, talking and living a la Bodeguita," states the record's liner notes, which continue, "Sepy has recently gained worldwide fame and notoriety through his celebrated nude statues in gold of Anita Ekberg and Jayne Mansfield. Besides rocking international art centers, his sculpting earned Sepy a very widely publicized sock in the nose from Anita's husband." Indeed, Sepy's reputation would follow him to Miami after the revolution, where, at his Coconut Grove bachelor pad, several of Linda Lovelace's notorious

RIGHT:
Havana remains a city of music with talented performers appearing in most bars, hotels, and restaurants.

BELOW:
Dos Hermanos Bar in Old Havana has been serving drinks for over one hundred years.

sex scenes in the X-rated hit *Deep Throat* were shot in 1972.

Near the piers and docks of Havana Vieja (Old Havana) were dozens of bars catering to sailors, stevedores, and anyone else wandering the area day or night. Among these, the Bar Dos Hermanos (Two Brothers Bar), already an institution by 1905, survives today with its long wooden bar and mirrored shelves of bottled rum.

Because Havana has always been a city of music, one didn't need to go far to be part of the scene. At almost every bar and restaurant was at least a *conjunto* (small musical group) performing traditional Afro-Cuban songs and popular American standards. For a city its size, Havana had perhaps the greatest number of talented musicians on earth.

Nightclubs and Cabarets

In the 1950s, Havana was the nightclub capital of the world. And atop Havana's nightclub pyramid were the Big Three: Montmartre, Sans Souci, and, at the apex, the fabulous Tropicana. Cuba's best musicians, dancers, and singers performed at the Big Three, where the pay and the prestige were the highest. These venues, which could seat over a thousand guests, were sprawling, multilayered affairs with cocktail lounges, full-service dinner menus, vast dance floors, one or two orchestras, dazzling cabaret revues, gift shops, and casinos. They put on two big shows a night, with the last performance often ending at 3:00 a.m. It was a labor-intensive business that provided work for many hundreds of Habaneros—the Tropicana alone employed over four hundred. In addition to the dozens of performers, there were waiters and waitresses, cooks, bartenders, costumers, stagehands, lighting technicians, croupiers, cashiers, cigarette girls, valets, janitors, and gardeners as well as the back-office business functions of bookkeeping and payroll. The clubs employed publicists and marketing men who created splashy ads for local and international magazines, touting big-name talent, as well as bus tour and convention coordinators. And there were kickbacks to be paid to tour operators, cabdrivers, hotel concierges, and the local politicians and police.

For the typical American, a visit to a Havana nightclub in 1958 was utterly transforming—an invitation to a forbidden, hedonistic world of rum, rumba, and roulette—and for many, an experience of a lifetime. It was the reason that tourists came to Cuba. Indeed, Havana's heady mix of tropical exoticism, sensual overload, and rum-fueled abandon existed nowhere else. Long before Las Vegas achieved its status as the premier playground for grown-ups, there was Havana. Because, back then, what happened in Havana stayed in Havana.

TWO BLOCKS FROM "HOTEL NACIONAL"

Montmartre

Havana   Cuba

MONTMARTRE

Montmartre

With its 1930s Streamline Moderne interior, Montmartre was situated on the third floor of a block-long neoclassical building in the heart of Havana's stylish Vedado district within walking distance of the hotels Nacional, Vedado, and the Habana Hilton. Montmartre's big fifty-person stage show, "Medianoche en Paris" ("Midnight in Paris"), starred the incandescent bombshells Zenia and Carlisse Novo, whose swivel-hipped dance routines set male audience members on fire. More sedate acts that were nonetheless crowd pleasers starred Maurice Chevalier and Dorothy Lamour, among many other popular performers. Typically there were three top-rated headliners whose performances rotated at any one time at Montmartre. As one of the big nightclubs that predated Batista's 1952 coup d'etat, the Montmartre, along with Sans Souci and Tropicana, had casino gambling to complement an

Habana Cuba

to an independent operator for a large fee and often taking a cut of the nightly take. At the Montmartre, Meyer Lansky held the club's gambling concession. For the winter season of 1951–52, Norman Rothman was the lessee of the Sans Souci's gaming tables—the season when the future of Havana's casinos was put in jeopardy by Rothman himself.

In April 1952, Dana C. Smith, an American tourist from California, lost $4,200 playing a crooked dice game known as razzle-dazzle at Rothman's Sans Souci casino. Smith, suspecting that he'd been cheated, stopped payment on a check he'd written to the casino to cover his losses. Cheekily, Norman Rothman sued Smith in a U.S. court to recover the funds. But Dana C. Smith was no ordinary tourist. He was a well-connected California attorney who upped the ante by loudly complaining about the incident to his close friend Senator (and soon-to-be vice president) Richard Nixon. With evidence provided by a helpful State Department, Smith proved that Havana's casinos were rife with crooked games, easily winning the case. The *Saturday Evening Post* got hold of the story and wrote a scathing investigative piece documenting how gullible Americans were being systematically fleeced at Cuba's casinos. The article concluded that only at the Montmartre, with its casino under the professional supervision of "mobster" Meyer Lansky, would a tourist find clean games of chance. President Batista, recognizing the damage that the story would have on Cuban tourism, quickly arrested and deported the razzle-dazzle scam artists. In addition, he hired Lansky as the government's advisor on

gambling reform to certify to the outside world that the games were on the up-and-up. Just as with Las Vegas, it was the mob that gamblers trusted to run a genuine game, and Meyer Lansky had built his career on that reputation. Following the razzle-dazzle debacle, shadowy Tampa, Florida–based gangster Santo Trafficante Jr. took over active control of the Sans Souci and, à la Lansky, kept his casino clean.

Several years later, Trafficante attempted to emulate the huge success of the Sans Souci's main rival, the dazzling Tropicana, by investing in a million-dollar expansion of his nightclub. Guests arriving for the 1956–57 season found the Sans Souci's previous outdoor stage replaced by multilevel circular platforms, each carrying elaborately costumed singers and dancers gyrating to the sounds of a live orchestra. To bring in the high rollers, Trafficante placed his enlarged Club Room casino under the well-publicized supervision of famed gambler "Lefty" Clark (William Bischoff) of Miami. With its big new casino and two "Spectacular Revues" that could seat over two thousand nightly, the Sans Souci became one of the obligatory stops for the popular "Night on the Town" bus tours in the last years of Batista's dictatorship. After the revolution, the swank Sans Souci became a military school.

ABOVE:
Sans Souci's spectacular new multilevel outdoor stage in 1957.

RIGHT:
Sans Souci *modelos* in "hats and diamonds" costumes.

Hotel Nightclubs

Following the passage of Batista's Hotel Law 2074 in 1955, which provided tax breaks and financing for new hotel/casino investments, each of Havana's big new American-owned hotels boasted its own magnificent showroom, cocktail lounge, fine restaurant, and casino. Modeled after Miami's Eden Roc and Fontainebleau and Las Vegas's mobbed-up Flamingo and Sands hotels, Havana's versions were just as brassy. Santo Trafficante's Hotel Capri had its deluxe showroom adjacent to the Casino de Capri. At Lansky's Havana Riviera, it was the Copa Room that brought in the crowds. The enormous Habana Hilton inaugurated its spacious El Caribe supper club in 1958. And the remodeled Hotel Nacional's Club Parisienne had two nightly cabaret shows that rivaled the Big Three in theatricality.

Havana's Other Nightclubs and Cabarets

As was true in nightclub scenes in New York, Chicago, Los Angeles, Paris, and elsewhere, there were the big, expensive and, by necessity, overly sanitized establishments where the cabarets' perceived vulgarity had been tamed for the tourist crowd. And then there were all the rest—the smaller, smoke-filled, densely packed clubs where the musicians, singers, and dancers were unrestrained. In Havana it was indeed in the dozens of smaller nightclub/cabarets located throughout the central city and suburbs where the cabaret as a musical genre evolved through experimentation and improvisation. It was where the musicians and the crowd could

LEFT:
Rudy and his partner in 1952.

ABOVE:
The legendary Ali Bar Club where Beny Moré became a star.

FACING, LEFT:
Casablanca's second show started at 3:00 a.m.

FACING, CENTER:
A glittering dance team between shows.

FACING, RIGHT:
Mr. Zombie welcomes you in 1946.

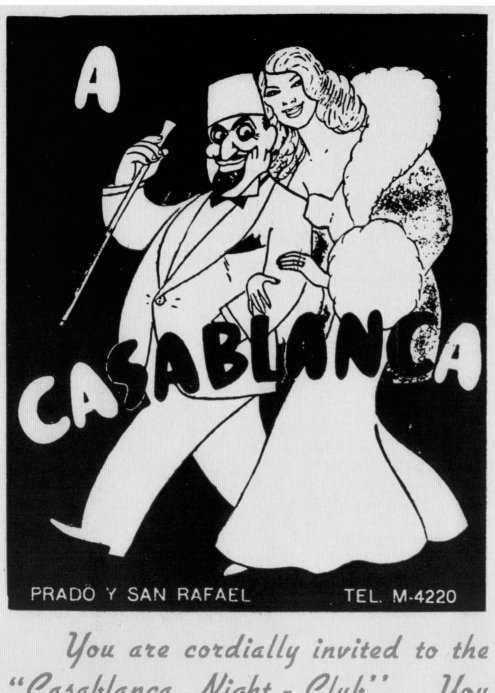

You are cordially invited to the "Casablanca Night - Club". You will enjoy one of the best shows in Havana. Two performances nightly 1:00 a. m. and 3:00 a. m.

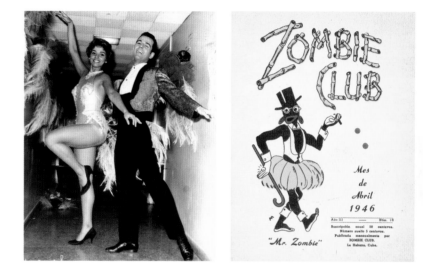

really swing. In the process, what filtered down from the Big Three to the second tier were the cabarets' elaborate costumes and choreography; what bubbled up were the musical innovations—the music's soul—that kept the high-end clubs from ossifying into boring repetition.

It was at the local clubs where performers were free to experiment and Habaneros could identify and nurture upcoming stars. One example was the Ali Bar on the city's outskirts where, in the early 1950s, Beny Moré's legendary performances led to his being crowned "El Barbaro del Ritmo" ("the Barbarian of Rhythm") as he became Cuba's biggest star. Others were scattered throughout the city, such as Casablanca and the Zombie Club near the Prado, and the Cabaret Pennsylvania, Panchin, and Rumba Palace out near the ocean in Marianao. Johnny's

Dream Club was located in Marianao, not far from the Tropicana. In addition to the Ali Bar there were other clubs situated along Rancho Boyeros Road out of town toward the airport, including Club Bambu, Topeka, Mulgoba, and Night and Day. In Havana's sophisticated Vedado district one found Johnny's 88 Club (under the same management as Johnny's Dream Club), Havana 1900 Nightclub, Mocambo, 21 Club, Club Las Vegas, and the Turf Club.

As in cities throughout Latin America and the world at that time, many of Havana's nightclubs were racially segregated, with those that were almost exclusively white and those that were frequented primarily by mulattoes and blacks—although whites could often be found at the black clubs in pursuit of the most "authentic" of the city's scenes. Additionally, there were small neighborhood clubs where all races generally mixed.

JOHNNY'S 88 CLUB

Calle O No. 208, Vedado.

Remembrance of wonder
at *Johnny's 8*

Johnny's DREAM CLUB

LEFT TO RIGHT:
The 21 Club featured "exotic décor"; Johnny's 88 Club and Johnny's Dream Club were popular local hangouts.

FACING:
Jumping for joy at Club Bambu.

For Havana's cabaret performers, as with such artists everywhere, their lives were nocturnal. With nightclubs letting out at 3:00 and 4:00 a.m. it was common for musicians, singers, and dancers to unwind at small restaurants and bars that wouldn't close until 8:00 a.m.—and not reopen until well after dark. As an all-encompassing way of life and as a means of earning a living, being a cabaret performer left little time for contemplating politics. For many, the revolutionary victory of 1959 came as a surprise. Soon, however, the new regime made it clear that

cabaret life was equated with the decadence of the Batista years, seeing it as unhealthy and unrevolutionary. Not only were the Big Three purged of their racier aspects, but the small neighborhood cabarets were also targeted and most of them dwindled away. The result was that by cleansing cabaret of its perceived depravity, the government ended up destroying much of what made Havana unique and alive. Only in recent years has the genre begun to reemerge as Cuba moves to embrace the totality of its cultural heritage.

Tropicana

"A Paradise under the Stars"

—Tropicana slogan

Tropicana was the world's most fabulous nightclub. The book *Tropicana Nights,* by historian Rosa Lowinger and Ophelia Fox (the late widow of Tropicana's visionary owner), is the definitive chronicle of the nightclub's history, from its origins as a Spanish Colonial–style estate to its status as the most exciting nightspot in Cuba.

The story begins in 1939, when Havana cabaret impresario Victor de Correa, owner of the phenomenally popular Eden Concert nightclub, was invited to partner with a pair of casino operators who had leased a large mansion situated on six lushly landscaped acres in the suburb of Marianao. Their idea was to convert the mansion into a

FAR RIGHT:
Three-tiered ritual sacrifice at Tropicana in 2007.

nightclub/casino. De Correa changed the property's name from Villa Mina (named after Doña Mina Pérez Chaumont, the estate's twice-widowed owner) to Tropicana, a combination of "tropical" and the last syllable of the owner's first name, "na."

Tropicana prospered until 1943, when German submarine attacks on local shipping ended tourist excursions to the island. With the loss of its American customers, Tropicana was virtually empty save for the action occurring at the two baccarat and monte tables rented by Martin Fox, a burly, gregarious, and well-connected Cuban gambler. Fox had emerged from the provinces four years earlier, where he had started out as a poor *guajiro* (rural peasant) who, through ambition and talent, became the master of the *bolitas* (illegal numbers lottery). Out of desperation, Tropicana's casino operators offered Fox the chance to purchase the establishment's entire casino concession—with Victor de Correa to remain in charge of the cabaret. Fox

agreed. However, with the election of the sanctimonious Ramón Grau San Martín as president in 1944, Tropicana's casino, as well as Sans Souci's and Montmartre's, were shut down, not reopening until the election of the more pragmatic Carlos Prío Socarrás in 1948.

Meanwhile, with the advent of mass tourism in the late 1940s and the increasing desire of middle-class Americans to travel, Havana had become a prime vacation destination. After 1948, Tropicana reaped this bounty as a popular nightspot for seeing a floor show and throwing money on the roulette

ABOVE:
Tropicana circa 1950 with its original logo and modest outdoor stage.

FAR LEFT:
Victor de Correa's popular Eden Concert nightclub circa 1938.

LEFT:
Tropicana's visionary new owner Martin Fox.

FACING:
Tropicana's ultramodern Arcos de Cristal (Crystal Arches) indoor cabaret in 1952.

tables, all in a romantic tropical garden setting. In 1950, Doña Mina finally sold her entire estate to Martin Fox, who had taken over the lease in 1943. Now, with the property under his control, Fox implemented the big plans that he had long nurtured, namely, the construction of an indoor cabaret that would allow performances to be given even in inclement weather. Fox hired the talented young Cuban architect Max Borges Jr. to implement his vision. The result was the magnificent Arcos de Cristal (Crystal Arches), a building so daring and

innovative that it would be one of only six Cuban designs to be featured in the New York Museum of Modern Art's book *Latin American Architecture Since 1945*. Wrote Tropicana historian Rosa Lowinger of Borges's design, "Using parabolic concrete arches and glass walls was the perfect complement for this garden setting, the perfect marriage of form and function—the credo of contemporary modernism. It was also a completely Cuban adaptation of the style, a space designed for the luxuriance of the tropics."

While the Arcos de Cristal was being built, the

increasingly sour relationship between Martin Fox and the cabaret's Victor de Correa finally came to a head, which led to a bitter severing of their business relationship and de Correa's departure with a sizeable cash payout. With de Correa out of the way, Fox's business partner Alberto Ardura was put in charge of finding a new choreographer for Tropicana's cabaret.

In Havana's cabaret scene, the talk of the 1952 season was a sensational new show appearing at the Sans Souci nightclub called "Sun Sun Babae," which was based on the mysterious Afro-Cuban Santería bembe

BELOW:
Plan of Tropicana's indoor and outdoor stages and game rooms.

RIGHT:
Sans Souci's "Sun Sun Babae" summoned a spellbound audience member (Skippy) to the stage.

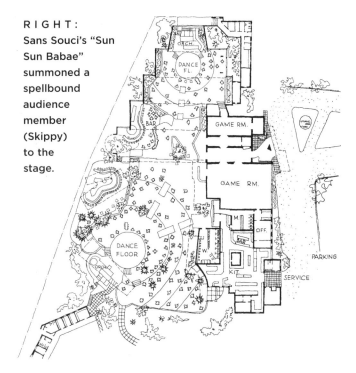

★ Olga CHAVIANO   ★ Celia CRUZ
★ ROCIO y ANTONIO   ★ and SKIPPY

ceremony furtively practiced throughout the country. Under the spell of rhythmic drumming and the chants of Santería priests, a member of Sans Souci's audience—a striking blond in a black satin cocktail dress—would be summoned in a trance to the stage, whereupon she would rip off her dress and join the line of dancers clad only in her underwear. Suddenly, after several dance numbers, the woman would be released from her trance, let loose an ear-piercing scream, frantically gather her scattered clothes, and flee the stage. Audiences went wild and the woman, in reality an American dancer named Skippy, would take her bows with the rest of the cast. The man responsible for this sensation was choreographer Roderico Neyra. Alberto Ardura had found the man to take over Tropicana's cabaret.

Once ensconced at Tropicana, Roderico Neyra, who went by the name Rodney, spent the next seven years creating the most astounding cabaret shows ever staged in Havana. A temperamental perfectionist who also happened to be gay, Rodney had been forced to end his career as a popular actor, singer, and dancer prematurely due to

the debilitating effects of leprosy that left his hands and feet painfully gnarled. Under the circumstances, it was amazing that Rodney was able to create and choreograph six to eight new back-to-back hit shows a season every year between 1952 and the revolution in 1959. Some of his most famous productions were the Afro-Cuban spectacles "Omelen-Ko," "Mayombe," and "Karabali;" "Europa Año Cero" (Europe, Year Zero), featuring famous characters from European history; the Hawaiian-themed

LEFT: Mercurial Rodney was the genius behind Tropicana's spectacular cabarets.

The themes of Rodney's Tropicana shows ranged from Afro-Cuban and Haitian voodoo rituals to Chinese, European, and Hawaiian spectacles, circus acts, and comedy revues.

OMELEN·KO
A TYPICAL VOODOO RITUAL...

voodoo *Ritual*
THIS IS CUBA, MISTER

TROPICANA **CONJUNTO SENEN SUAREZ**
CUBAN RHUMBA BAND FEATURED DAILY AT TROPICANA ★

"A Paradise Under the Stars"

Cuban music and native African rhythms find their true expression in Tropicana's shows.

The OMELEN-KO -a negro baptism- is one of the most fascinating productions staged at Tropicana. The frenzied rhythms of a *lucumí* ritual, expressed by the tam-tam of the *Batá* drums; the *Illá*, the *Okónkolo* and the *Itósteles*, played by real members of this African faith.

La música típica cubana y los ritmos afros se presentan en Tropicana con el mayor apego a sus tradiciones y a su liturgia.

El OMELEN-KO -bautizo negro- es uno de los más impresionantes shows presentados. Un rito lucumí típico de una religión que se expresa en el tamtam de los tambores batá: el Illá, el Okónkolo y el Itósteles, que fueron tocados por verdaderos miembros de esta secta.

"Polynesia;" "El Circo" ("The Circus") which utilized lions and an elephant; and "This is Cuba, Mister," a raucous comedy revue. Backing the performances and providing dance music between floor shows were two top orchestras—Armando Romeu Jr. and the Conjunto Senen Suarez, plus a famous continental guest band.

Soon after the completion of Arcos de Cristal and the hiring of Rodney, Max Borges Jr. finished the installation of an enormous geometric metal sculpture that covered the Bajo Las Estrellas (Under the Stars) outdoor stage and was itself a multilevel platform for the show's costumed *modelos* (models), singers, and dancers. The dramatically lit elliptical

CLOCKWISE FROM ABOVE:
Under the Stars in 1952. Tropicana's swank entrance area. Keeping an eye on the action at Tropicana.

Thankfully, not much has changed at Tropicana in the fifty-plus years between 1954 (left) and 2007 (above). Architect Max Borges Jr.'s outdoor metal sculpture/stage continues to dazzle audiences.

Gamba's famous dancing nymphs marble fountain, which had welcomed patrons to the Casino Nacional since the 1910s, was purchased by Martin Fox and installed in Tropicana's entrance gardens when the old casino was closed because of competition from the big nightclubs.

sculpture was actually a three-dimensional representation of a complex mathematical formula, according to the architect.

In addition to its signature architectural triumphs, Tropicana's icon was its twirling ballerina designed by Rita Longa for the nightclub in 1950. The figure, which stood in a small reflecting pool near the entrance of the Crystal Arch room, appeared on brochures, cardboard table stands, swizzle sticks, and tableware, and centered the Club Room's roulette wheels. Two years later, in 1952, Aldo

Due to its place atop Havana's nightclub hierarchy, Tropicana attracted Cuba's greatest performing talents to its stages, including Celia Cruz, Olga Guillot, Celeste Mendoza, and Beny Moré. Nat King Cole was an enormous draw when he appeared at Tropicana, as were Josephine Baker and Carmen Miranda. And topping the club's guest list over the years were Ernest Hemingway, Ava Gardner, Marlon Brando, Liberace, Joan Crawford, Debbie Reynolds, Elizabeth Taylor, and Cesar Romero. Mexican film star Evangelina Elizondo starred in the 1957 Mexican

CLOCKWISE FROM LEFT:
Cover of Tropicana's big twenty-six-page illustrated souvenir booklet. Dancing nymphs casino chip. The twirling ballerina, Tropicana's enduring icon, centers the roulette wheel.

FACING:
The 1957 Mexican film *Tropicana* depicted the nightclub in all its splendor.

romantic comedy *Tropicana*, shot on location at the nightclub, which included a guest performance by the famous Mexican composer Agustín Lara.

One of the nightclub's more sensational promotions was the weekly Tropicana Special charter flight aboard Cubana Airlines' Lockheed Constellation from Miami to Havana, inaugurated in 1956. By removing eight seats and installing a six-foot stage, proscenium, and curtain, the passenger cabin was transformed into a mini-version of Tropicana's Crystal Arch showroom. Backed by five costumed musicians, Tropicana's acrobatic dance team, Ana Gloria and Rolando, put on a lively

show involving singing, dancing, and passenger participation culminating in a riotous conga line down the middle of the aisle. *Cabaret* magazine's January 1957 issue gushed of Ana Gloria, "Some of the lucky males find their hair mussed, their cheek patted as she passes, and some return the favor. A few find her in their laps, smiling impishly and bounding out again before they regain their wits." The Tropicana Special was just the kick-off to

a Havana holiday that, for $68.80, included the flight, Tropicana's dinner show, an overnight stay in a Havana hotel, breakfast, and a return flight.

> Good fortune may smile at Tropicana—in the glittering Club Room. Perhaps at the dizzy whirl of the roulette, the turn of the card at chemin de fer [baccarat], when dice roll or the chuck-a-luck wheel spins. It's fun! It's exciting! It's at Tropicana!
> — Tropicana brochure, 1953

Fox wanted to give his Club Room casino customers the same indoor-outdoor garden experience as his Crystal Arch room, so in 1954 the casino was moved to an entirely new modern glassed-in space, where lit palms and views of the nymph fountain complemented the green felt of the craps tables.

FACING AND ABOVE: Ana Gloria and Rolando's teaser show aboard the weekly Tropicana Special flight from Miami to Havana.

RIGHT: The Club Room casino before moving to its modern new glass-roofed space.

119

Havana at Night

"Havana at night is a glittering jewel set in the black velvet of the Caribbean. She is a seductive sorceress exuding an essence of warmth and indolence and delicious lethargy. Her streets throb with a dark and pulsating beat. The air is a heavy, aphrodisiacal wine that dissolves the inhibitions and dissipates restraint. The tourist is caught in a heady torrent of rich laughter and swept along in swirling freshets of gaiety. The music is everywhere. Time is an endless round of dark rum and rhumba, light rum and marimbas, for Havana is the mistress of pleasure, the lush and opulent goddess of delights."

—Jay Mallin, *Cabaret Quarterly*, 1956

"Everything's legal in Havana"

—Jim Wormold, protagonist of Graham Greene's
Our Man in Havana, 1959

As one of the New World's oldest port cities, Havana has long been known for the vices offered sailors on leave. By the late nineteenth century, prostitution near the docks had become especially rampant where, on warm nights, ladies appeared in the open windows of the many nearby houses along narrow colonial streets. Following independence in 1902 and during its six decades as a republic, Cuba experienced periodic, generally half-hearted reform movements that attempted to reign in the sex trade—but to no avail. When crackdowns hit one area of Havana, activity would reappear in another.

During America's 1920s Prohibition era, Havana's close proximity to the United States led to a burgeoning tourist industry centered on free-flowing alcohol and other pleasures, such as exotic cabaret shows, rumba bands, and the ever-present temptations of the flesh. For help in navigating this convenient but foreign land, the popular *Terry's Guide to Cuba* by the intrepid travel writer T. Philip Terry offered insights into Cuba's history, its must-see destinations, hotel ratings, and street maps. The 1929 edition of the book also included a short section titled "Night Life." In it, Terry identified "a rather indecorous quarter" in Old Havana bounded by Calle de Economica, Calle de la Merced, and the old wharves. Here "in this confessedly naughty ward are tapestried and mirrored rooms where the salaciously inclined may witness startling scenes in the flesh or by means of moving pictures. Such places are usually referred to by the cryptic number soixante-neuf (in Spanish, *sesenta y nueve,* or 69) albeit this number is not that

ABOVE:
U.S. sailors on leave during World War II, one of whom has found himself a date.

LEFT:
A business card for the seedy Paris Bar in Guantanamo Bay.

PARIS BAR

THE BEST OF THE BEST IN GUANTANAMO BAY
A NICE PLACE FOR A GOOD TIME
AVERYTHING IS DOWN STAIRS, WALK IN NEXT DOOR OF THE PRO STATION.
FROM HELL TO HAVEN AND FROM HAVEN TO HELL
LOOK THIS CARD ON THE BACK.
DRINKS. — GIRLS. — MUSIC.

of the houses in question." He also noted the variety of available women "varying in complexion from peach white to coal black; 15-year-old flappers and ebony antiques . . . who unblushingly loll about heavy-eyed and languorous . . . studiously displaying

their physical charms or luring the stranger by flaming words or maliciously imperious gestures." After cautioning about the risk of catching communicable diseases, Terry concluded the section by recommending the safer, more brightly lit district near the Prado promenade where the chief irritant was the persistent touts (pimps).

Cuba's political upheavals of the 1930s, combined with the end of Prohibition and the advent of the Great Depression, cut deeply into the American tourist trade. The early 1940s once again brought waves of Americans—this time hot-blooded sailors stopping at Havana's port of call during World War II. But it wasn't until after Batista's 1952 coup that Havana emerged as the world's top destination for sex tourism and a harbinger of what would appear in Saigon, Bangkok, and Manila in the 1960s. Batista's laissez-faire attitude toward Havana's expanding sex industry was consistent with his strong support of casino gambling—it brought American tourists to Cuba.

Havana's brothels were clustered in the residential blocks west of the city center's lower Prado—the wide, tree-lined promenade that led from the imposing Capitolio building to the seaside Malecón. Conveniently, the Prado was also the locus of the central city's best tourist hotels such as the Inglaterra, the Sevilla-Biltmore, and

LEFT:
Pimp and prostitute grace the cover of Cuba's *Carteles* magazine in 1937.

CLOCKWISE FROM ABOVE:
A Cuban men's magazine. The 1956 *Cabaret Quarterly* exposed Havana's seamy underbelly. The former red-light district on Calle Colón (Colón Street) in 2007.

the Plaza. In the early 1950s, a brief walk from one's hotel lobby would lead to a sordid and rowdy red-light district of battered old buildings known as the Colón Quarter (Calles Colón, Bernal, Virtudes, and Trocadero). Among those documenting Havana's side streets and sleazy underbelly after World War II were writers for popular men's magazines such as Cuba's *Gente* and America's *Stag* and *Cabaret*.

Of the notorious Colón Quarter, *Stag* magazine noted at the time that "chattering, cajoling women lean out the lower windows [of the area] 24 hours a day. Plucking at your clothes, the women bluntly advertise their wares. Their English is rudimentary but specific. 'One dollar! One dollar!' emerges loud and understandable from the welter of Spanish jabbering." However, around 1950, Cuba's Prío administration embarked upon a flicker of reform, causing the authorities to clear the Colón Quarter of its brothels and freelance streetwalkers. While respectable tenants quickly occupied the now-vacant and highly desirable old buildings, the former dwellers reestablished themselves in new locations farther from the center, such as the suburban Vedado district nearby.

In many of the city's small, less reputable taverns, "B-girls"—bargirls employed by bar owners to act as companions to male customers—entertained the tourists. In addition, some of these bars operated as fronts for harder-edged gals who led their clients to concealed back rooms and upper floors of the narrow buildings. One such joint was the 212 Bar-Club, where the backlit sign of a woman's seductive long-lashed eye was a signal to those in the know. Not to be left out, female tourists were free to accept the entreaties of slick-haired Cuban gigolos who frequented the tourist areas, ready to give an American secretary a robust weekend of Latin love.

Competition among the city's bordellos led one enterprising proprietor, whose Hotel Chic was located in Havana's notorious Chinatown district, to distribute promotional cards with the establishment's address and list of amenities on one side and three-dimensional photos of seminude women cavorting in their boudoirs on the reverse—complete with 3-D glasses for witnessing the full effect.

212 Bar Club Then and Now

For their first taste of naughty Havana, sailors on leave during World War II and afterward headed straight to Cabaret Kursaal. Conveniently situated directly across from the piers, Kursaal advertised itself as a "Tipical Cuban Palace" with red-hot nightly revues at 1:00 and 3:00 a.m. featuring "Living Pictures" and a dance team that, according to *Stag* magazine in 1950, "does the rhumba the way its creators made it—an African mating dance." Said the magazine, "If you take a table alone, you are swarmed by elaborately sexy women before you can order a drink. If your wife or girl is along, the Cuban B-girls move in anyway."

ABOVE:
The 212 Bar Club was a front for a small brothel. In 2007 it housed an entire family.

VISITE EL

HOTEL "CHIC"

ULTIMA CREACION · DISCRETO · ECONOMICO

No es uno más en su clase, es el único.
Todo fabricado especialmente para crear
el Hotel CHIC. - Baños en todas las habitaciones con abundante agua fria y caliente.
Mobiliario Confortable.

SIEMPRE ABIERTO

Telf. M-9031 - Rayo 213, entre Reina y Salud

HOTEL CHIC
EL MEJOR SITUADO
RECIEN INAUGURADO
HABITACIONES EN
QUE SE SENTIRA COMO
EN NOCHE DE BODAS

M-9031 RAYO, 213
entre
REINA Y SALUD

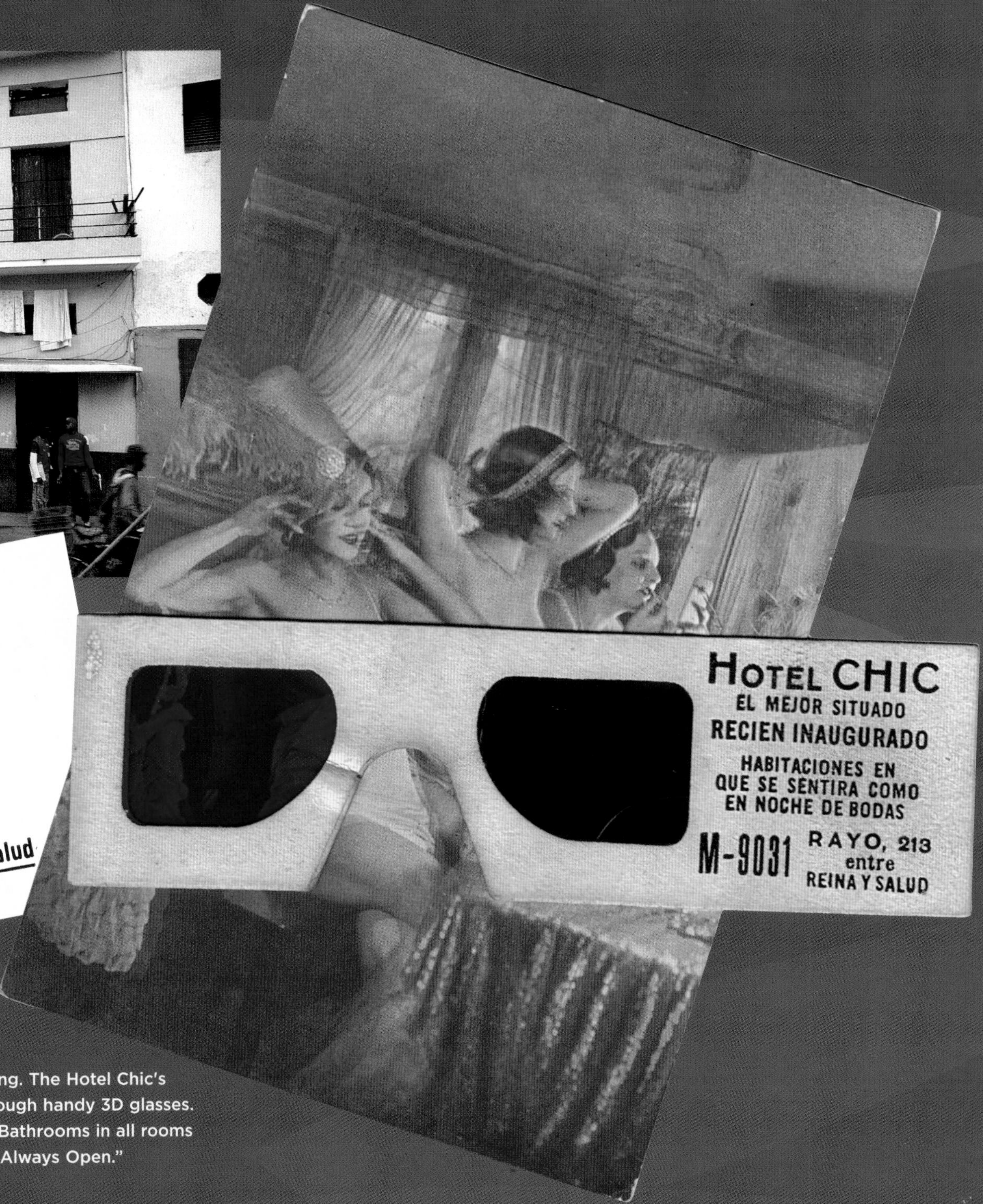

CLOCKWISE FROM TOP LEFT:
Former Hotel Chic brothel in 2007, now an apartment building. The Hotel Chic's
1950s-era promotional card featured topless gals visible through handy 3D glasses.
Hotel Chic: "Discrete, affordable, not one better in its class. Bathrooms in all rooms
with abundant cold and hot water. Comfortable furnishings. Always Open."

CABARET
KURSAAL
NIGHT CLUB.   TIPICAL CUBAN PALACE
4   PAULA   ST.
TELEPHONE M-5455
HAVANA, CUBA

Among middle- and upper-class Habaneros, it was considered a rite of passage by some that teenage boys lose their virginity in one of the city's better brothels. Among such establishments, the Mambo Club was highly regarded. Located on the outskirts of the city along the airport highway, the Mambo Club gave the impression of an upscale Havana nightclub with its orchestra, dance floor surrounded by tables, and bar. However, once you were seated, one or more beautiful women would join you at your table to playfully converse. After several daiquiris and, perhaps, a vulgar dance or two to a rumba beat, you would surrender ten pesos to a door-guarding matron and be led through a maze of corridors to one of many small rooms. Under a mirrored

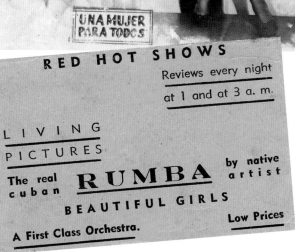

HOT PUSSY!

BUT COLD FEET

RED HOT SHOWS

Reviews every night at 1 and at 3 a.m.

LIVING PICTURES

The real cuban RUMBA by native artist

BEAUTIFUL GIRLS

A First Class Orchestra.   Low Prices

ABOVE LEFT AND RIGHT:
A late-1940s burlesque show lobby card promising "A woman for all."

LEFT:
Cabaret Kursaal's crude business card folded in just such a way for the visual joke to work.

RIGHT:
The Mambo Club in 2007. It once was Havana's most upscale nightclub/brothel, popular with Habaneros.

BELOW:
Another lobby card.

LOWER RIGHT:
American Betty Howard bumps and grinds at a Havana club in 1956.

your carnal hostess would be back working the bar within the half-hour.

Of all of Havana's brothels, Casa Marina was widely recognized as the most palatial. By way of Spain, Doña Marina had established herself in post-war Havana as the Queen of the Madams in a large two-story residence prominently located on the corner of Twenty-Fifth Street and the seaside Malecón in the city's fashionable Vedado district. *Stag* writer Robert Fortune described Marina's castlelike bordello with its white-coated servants as sumptuously decorated with plush draperies and period furniture "in the tradition of the old French 'maison de joie.' She cultivates a cosmopolitan atmosphere providing French, Chinese, and American girls as well as native lasses." He noted that "Marina's crowning service is rarely offered in

ceiling the long anticipated act would be consummated. And, as was common with the newly initiated,

Aunt Nena welcomed visitors in English and Spanish.

Cuba or anywhere. Two trained nurses stand by from dawn to dawn in a spotlessly clean 'clinic' to guard the health of customer and employee alike."

Legendary English travel writer Graham Greene, who, as a carousing night crawler in the mid-1950s, sought out Havana's seamiest venues, was quite familiar with the Mambo Club, Casa Marina, and the city's rawest cabarets. In his book *Ways of Escape*, Greene wrote, "I enjoyed the louche atmosphere of Batista's city and I never stayed long enough to become aware of the sad political background of arbitrary imprisonment and torture. I came there for the brothel life, the roulette in every hotel, the fruit machines spilling out jackpots of silver dollars, the Shanghai Theatre

RIGHT: Havana's top madam Doña Marina built her palatial bordello, seen here in 2007, right on the seaside Malecón in chic Vedado.

ABOVE TOP:
Author Graham Greene frequented Havana's naughtiest venues.

ABOVE:
Shanghai Theatre proprietor Jose Orozco Garcia outside his establishment.

RIGHT:
Buying a ticket for Shanghai's burlesque show and stag films.

where for one dollar 25 cents one could see a nude cabaret of extreme obscenity."

The Shanghai Theatre of which Greene refers was without doubt the most infamous burlesque house in Havana. Located on Calle Zanja, a major thoroughfare and a short walk from Havana's most respectable downtown shopping streets, the Shanghai was a shabby old Chinatown relic of 750 seats that *Cabaret* magazine called "the naughtiest theatre in the world" in 1956. Featuring risqué plays, raw burlesque, and stag movies, its 9:30 and 11:30 p.m. shows were packed with tourists, especially on Saturday nights. Seated in creaking, uncomfortable chairs in the hot airless theatre, closely packed patrons would witness a performance where, *Cabaret* reported,

> flimsy under-garments disappear until the spectators behold a dizzy picture of completely naked women gyrating, bumping and twisting in a way that drops all theatrical pretense and concentrates on thrusting the impulses of nature alone across the Shanghai footlights. Like a nudist camp gone berserk they throw themselves nearer and nearer to the customers until a frenzied pace is reached. Then, as if to spare the hearts of the older members of the audience, the curtain closes mercifully on the fast-moving spectacle.

Next, a movie screen would be lowered and pornographic movies projected to the overheated audience. A scene in the film version of Graham Greene's *Our Man in Havana,* which was shot on location in Havana on the eve of the 1959 revolution, documents

the sordid flavor of the Shanghai. In the movie, vacuum cleaner salesman-turned-British spy Jim Wormold (Alec Guinness) goes to the theatre during a burlesque performance that was obviously sanitized for its motion picture audience.

Another of Havana's naughtier nightspots was the Palette Club, situated out of town along Havana's Central Highway, which was famous for its drag shows and private rooms where pornographic films were shown.

In his attempt at re-creating Havana's lurid fleshpots, Francis Ford Coppola included a scene in his 1974 film *Godfather Part II* in which mob boss Michael Corleone and several associates of Hyman Roth are taken to a raunchy sex show. Standing

near the back of the crowded smoke-filled theatre, they witness a strapping youth on stage theatrically drop his red velvet cloak before a rapturous female as he reveals his prodigious manhood. In 1950s Havana, the actual star of that show was a handsome Cuban mulatto who performed under the stage name "Superman," with an international reputation derived from possessing a penis that, when erect, was reportedly the length of a line of twelve silver dollars.

For millions of American moviegoers, Coppola's film left the impression that Batista's Havana in the late 1950s was nothing more than a debauched, mob-infested playground with its deluxe veneer being stripped away by the growing revolution. As much as this simplistic view has persisted, life in Havana at that time was—as with any major world city—exceptionally diverse and complex, with many layers, of which its vices were perhaps more in evidence than most.

During the booming postwar years, many Americans of note found their way to Havana. In addition to stars of the entertainment world such as Frank Sinatra, Nat King Cole, and Liberace, important politicians were spotted in the old Spanish city. Prior to his election as president in 1960, Senator John F. Kennedy took a short vacation to Havana with his colleague, Florida senator George Smathers, in December 1957. In addition to enjoying rounds of golf, sailing, and visits to the city's fabulous nightclubs, Kennedy did not ignore the more

RIGHT:
Can you spot the Palette Club's female impersonators in this festive group shot?

RIGHT:
Bobby de Castro was one of Havana's top female impersonators before fleeing to San Francisco after the revolution.

sensual aspects of Havana's nightlife. In his biography of mobster Meyer Lansky, who was the most prominent of the American gamblers running Havana's big casinos in the 1950s, journalist Robert Lacey reports a conversation that Lansky had with his attorney in the 1970s about Kennedy's 1957 Cuba trip:

> Everyone in the business knew that Kennedy had a voracious sexual appetite, Lansky confided disapprovingly. The senator pursued women with a recklessness which was extraordinary in someone entrusted with a public office.

Historian Rosalie Schwartz summarized the time period: "In the transitional era between the clumsy groping of the drive-in movie and the boastful sexuality of the hot tub, Cuba offered tourists an acceptable way to succumb to temptation without scandalizing the neighbors."

Laura Aguiler

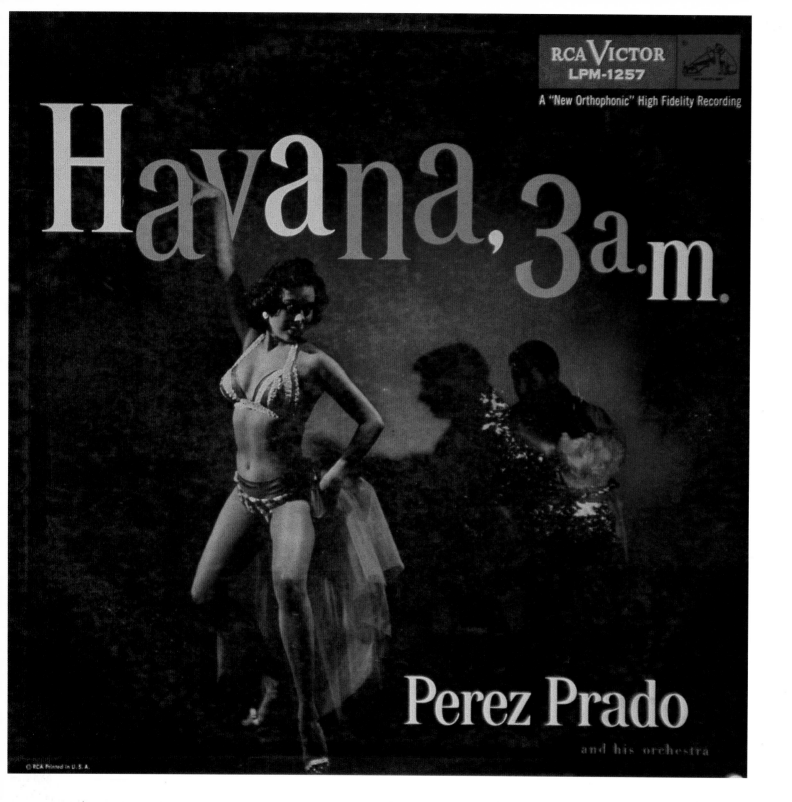

LEFT:
It seems Havana's witching hour was not midnight but 3:00 a.m.

A Man on the Make

It's January 17, 1958, and you're an unmarried thirty-six-year-old ad exec catching Pan Am's flight 442 from New York to Havana, arriving at 6:00 p.m. on a Friday night. After checking into the flashy new Hotel Capri in the city's stylish Vedado district you freshen up, dress up (tan linen suit, snazzy tie, polished shoes) and catch the elevator to the Capri's rooftop lounge to sample one of those famous Cuban drinks, perhaps a daiquiri or a mojito. A musical trio plays "The Breeze and I" and "Siboney" before taking a break — the signal for you to go back down to the air-conditioned lobby and into the humid tropical night air. A cabbie suggests La Floridita, which you've heard about, as a fine place for a meal. "Cradle of the daiquiri, huh?" It's good, too. And so is the lobster thermidor. The maitre d' offers you a Montecristo Number 2 cigar, the one that looks like a torpedo, which you accept. Smoking Havana cigars takes time, so you pay the bill and wander outside in the direction of the Malecón, passing Sloppy Joe's Bar (looks crowded) and the back of the Sevilla-Biltmore, where you can hear laughter and Cuban music drifting from the hotel's roof garden restaurant.

Girls and touts appear from the shadows whispering inducements; but you've decided on a different route for tonight. Cigar finished, you take a taxi to the 212 Bar-Club on Consulado Street, a place a work buddy recommended. It's a bit lowbrow, but there are plenty of girls at the bar — a couple of them real lookers — and they're dressed decent enough for going out to a show. One of them, her name seems to be Juana or Wanda or something like that, is real friendly, sort of a Cuban Jayne Mansfield. Not really. But she's got nice curves and platinum blonde hair and she laughs a lot. Her English isn't so great, but who cares? You can communicate. There's a small band playing the cha-cha-chá so you both dance a little bit (thank you Arthur Murray) and sip daiquiris at your table. Damn good, those daiquiris — hats off to Hemingway. But you've got big plans for the evening and it's time for you and Juana (or Wanda) to head out for the Sans Souci nightclub's second cabaret show. The one that starts at midnight and goes until 2:00 or 3:00 a.m.

It's a twenty-minute taxi ride, but it's okay 'cause you're snuggled in the back seat. By the time you get there the show's already started. No matter. It's quite a place — outdoors with hundreds of tables that circle a great big multilevel stage. A decent orchestra. You get a table near the back. The show has lots of good-looking gals with plenty of thigh and pleasing backsides and knockers to boot. But you're too busy with each other to pay much attention to all of that. She says she wants to play a little roulette, so you wander over to the Club Room (air conditioned, thank God) and watch her jiggle as she wins on number thirty-three. That doesn't last long and you figure it's time for one last mojito (or two) in the Nevada cocktail lounge before heading back to the Capri.

As you enter the hotel lobby — it's real late — the lobby clerk barely looks up as you guide Juana/Wanda to the elevators and room 728. Yep, and you've got one more night to kill in this town. Not bad.

Life
as a Habanero

ABOVE LEFT:
Dominoes, a popular pastime for Cubans.

ABOVE RIGHT:
A typical fruit-peddler's cart.

FACING:
Celebrating the opening of the Minimax supermarket in 1954 with a round of cocktails.

For the average Habanero (resident of Havana) in the 1950s, the city was alive in every respect. While Cuban politics roiled in the background (and sometimes in the foreground), Habaneros went on with living. A typical day began with the lyrical voices of street vendors singing their wares—mangos, guayabas, plantains, papayas—as they wandered Havana's streets. In the Spanish

tradition, breakfast was light—bread or pastry and strong coffee, often taken at the local café where friends would meet before going to work. Lunch, however, was heavy, typically consisting of Cuba's national dish—*arroz con frijoles* (rice and beans)—soup, a meat course, plantains, dessert, fruit in season, and coffee. Always coffee. Then a short siesta and back to work.

An overwhelming variety of street smells also defined Havana, especially in the hot tropical summer months—fried steaks, spicy Cuban hamburgers, baked breads, coffee—all made more pungent by the general lack of air conditioning. Add to that the

singing peddlers, buses, rumbling American cars, pedestrians, and the sounds of Cuban music radiating from bars, restaurants, homes, and passing cars, and a rich vibrancy of street life, work life, and home life was created.

After work and a meal, Habaneros would sometimes play dominoes or socialize with friends and family at home, on verandas, on porch steps, at cafés or bars, and also at clubs and cabarets. Indeed, tourists were not the only ones enjoying Havana's exciting nightlife—Cubans were having fun at these venues, too.

In striving for a middle-class lifestyle, Habaneros took their cues from the United States, driving American cars and choosing single-family homes stocked with the latest American appliances in Havana's suburbs. They shopped at the big Havana department stores, the most prestigious of which was the Macy's-like El Encanto that occupied an entire city block, and Fin de Siglo, both located in the heart of the city's crowded shopping district. It was here, at the "corner of sin," the intersection of San Rafael and Galiano streets west of the Prado, where young men gathered to watch bare-shouldered perfumed young women in fashionable dresses walk by.

LEFT:
Busy Calle Neptuno (Neptuno Street).

ABOVE:
Stoking the consumer culture in 1956.

Studebaker EL AUTO IDEAL

WASHINGTON AVE. MOTOR Co.

AVE. DE WASHINGTON No. 135   LA HABANA

This is El Encanto

your store in Havana

Havana's middle class

took its cues from America. El Encanto (lower left) was the city's most prestigious department store, followed by Fin de Siglo (left, as seen in 2007). El Encanto was destroyed by arson in 1961.

FACING:
"Celebrating the Progress of Our City" with a 1951 Cadillac grand prize.

BELLA LA SALVAJE

LEFT:
Voluptuous Blanquita Amaro was one of Cuba's most popular film stars.

ABOVE:
Blanquita Amaro stars in *The Beautiful Savage*, shot in Cuba and Equatorial Guinea in 1953.

RIGHT:
Bodybuilding competition in Havana.

BELOW:
The champion Club Habana baseball team.

For Cubanos, the most seductive and desirable of all movie stars was the voluptuous vedette and diva Blanquita Amaro, who represented the ideal Cuban woman with her hourglass figure and tempestuous nature.

Another enduring American import was baseball, introduced to Cuba by United States military forces stationed on the island during the 1898 Spanish-American War and subsequent four-year occupation. Cuba, having taken to baseball in a big way, developed intense rivalries between the island's fourteen

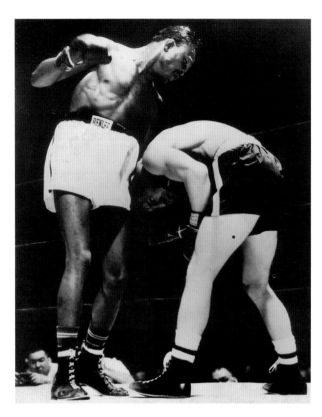

2018 Cuban Cock Fight.

teams, the most passionate of which was between "Los Rojos" ("The Reds") of Club Habana, with a lion as their mascot, and "Los Azules" ("The Blues") of Almendares, with a scorpion as their talisman. Cuban baseball historians Mark Rucker and Peter C. Bjarkman write: "The two baseball clubs were at the very heart of the city's sporting and social life and passions ran equally as deep among their rabid followers as they ever did between devotees of Brooklyn and New York big-league clubs during the same epoch." Similarly, boxing emerged as a hugely popular sport during this time period, with Cuban champions fighting major bouts in the capital that attracted both local and international audiences. Pre-Republic entertainments such as cockfighting

and jai alai (a fast-paced indoor sport of Basque origin) retained their popularity. Cockfighting was especially popular among the poor.

Another ubiquitous Cuban obsession was playing the national lottery (*bolita*), which evolved into a daily event during the Batista years with multimillion peso prizes—and fantastic kickbacks to the president and his cronies. From cockfights and jai alai to the lottery, Cubans were indeed incessant gamblers.

As a nominally Catholic country, Cuba retained elements of the religion's prudishness inherited from the island's Spanish past. Until the middle of the twentieth century, it was not uncommon for courtships to be conducted through the grilled windows

Cuba's national lottery, or *bolita,* became a daily obsession during Batista's reign. An April 1958 lottery ticket celebrates Sputnik's successful launch.

The National Lottery is part and parcel of Cuban life. Tickets are sold at dozens of stands like this where patrons choose a favorite number—frequently based on a dream.

Cuban Courtship.

of colonial-era dwellings. In the postwar period, car outings, movies, dinner dates, and evening strolls along the Malecón continued to be chaperoned by family members.

In February or March of each year, Havana celebrated carnival with an enthusiasm rivaling Rio de Janeiro and New Orleans. A parade of elaborate motorized floats piled with costumed revelers traveled down the Prado and Malecón, followed by musicians and dancers, many of whom were members of venerable clubs—such as La Sultana, El Alacrán, and La Jardinera—whose flamboyant costumes and choreographed routines were all-year projects. A uniquely Cuban element of carnival was the towering *farola,* or pole lantern, deftly balanced by parading dancers. The final judging of the club entries occurred at the large colonial-era Centro Asturiano building in the heart of the city.

Many Cubans saw no contradiction in celebrating carnival, the advent of the Christian Lent, and participating in the ceremonies of Santería, a religion that originated in Cuba during the island's centuries of slavery. Indeed, Santería evolved as a melding of Spanish Catholicism and West African religious traditions. In Santería worship, Catholic saints double as orishas (spiritual emissaries), one of the most powerful being Babalu Aye—Saint Lazarus—who cures illnesses and heals infectious diseases. It was Babalu Aye of whom Desi Arnaz sang while beating his conga drum in American nightclubs, bedazzling a cocktail crowd oblivious of the song's Santería origins. Santería ceremonies were practiced primarily in secret until the late twentieth century, when the religion came out of the shadows as an accepted part of Cuban life.

In escaping Havana's summer heat, the wealthy retreated to their Varadero villas or the swank

LEFT:
Courtship rituals in the old days.

FACING:
Outlandish costumes and towering *farolas* marked carnival in Havana.

You'll Be Happy In Havana

Dancer carrying spectacular "farola"—lantern—and young people in festooned car are typical of Havana's Carnival.

Habana: Comparsa de Carnaval. Carnival Scene.

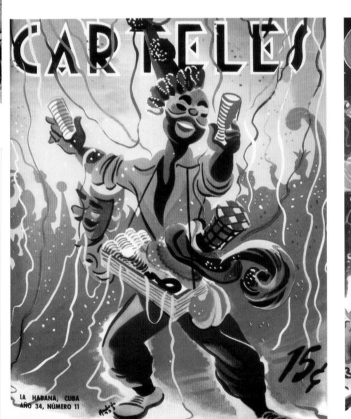

Cubans and American Cars

Cuba's enduring obsession with American cars goes back to when Ford's Model T began appearing on Havana's streets in the 1910s. Given America's dominant role in Cuba's economy and its close proximity to the island, it was natural that American cars became ubiquitous throughout the republic.

Virtually every make and model that came off Detroit's assembly lines appeared in Havana—until 1960. The American trade embargo that followed Castro's revolution halted the export of American cars (and car parts) to the island. Desperate to keep their treasured Chevy Bel Airs, Buick LeSabres, Dodge Kingsways, and Cadillac Sevilles running, Cubans have been forced to become the world's most resourceful mechanics, fashioning parts out of scrap metal and fusing together rusted side panels with layers of bondo. Entire extended families continue to pack into these rumbling, brightly painted dinosaurs with their dim headlights and gray exhaust belching from rusted tailpipes. And yet, compared with the pathetic tin-can Ladas imported from the Soviet Union in the sixties and seventies, American cars remain cherished family members that continue to be nursed in defiance of the laws of nature.

Ford and Lincoln dealership circa 1929

1948 Frazer Manhattan

1958 Dodge Kingsway

A line of beauties near the Capitolio

The main drag in Pinar del Rio

1947 Chevrolet Fleetline

1959 Buick

Cuba's Incredible Music Scene

"One of your most durable impressions of Cuba will be the music you hear. In the typical Cuban music of the 'son' and 'danzon'—now become so popular in the States—you can distinguish dulcet melodic progressions of Spain and the compelling tom-tom rhythms of Africa. The result is sensuous and exciting. To American ears attuned to the equally barbaric tempos of jazz, the Cuban variety of syncopation is a pleasant and stimulating change. Wherever you go in Cuba you will hear these distinctive popular songs—whether in the glittering ballroom of an elite casino, hotel or club or in the patio of a country tavern."

— Cuban tourist guidebook, 1931

The influence of Cuban music on twentieth-century American popular culture has been extraordinary. Yet until the 1930s, the Caribbean island had been represented musically in the United States by novelty tunes such as "Cuban Moon" and Irving Berlin's "I'll See You in C – U – B – A."

The roots of most Cuban musical forms lie in the melding of West African rhythms with Spanish melodies that began in the sixteenth century with the arrival of slaves to work the island's sugar and coffee plantations. Added to this Afro-Spanish broth were French Creole influences such as the country dance (*contradanza*) brought by Haitians

RIGHT:
The popular Orquesta Aragón.

158

Popular novelty tunes of the 1920s preceded America's infatuation with the Cuban rumba.

(white and black) fleeing that island's revolution around 1800.

It is believed that Cuban maracas (seed-filled rattles) are the only remaining musical legacy of the island's indigenous Taíno and Siboney peoples, who were wiped out by the invading Spanish in the 1500s. From Africa came percussive instruments such as the clave (high-pitched sticks) and conga and bata drums. Spain contributed the guitar, the piano, and other classical European instruments. From these instruments and influences emerged the

Cuban *danzón*, *son*, and *guajira*, along with their associated dances. In the twentieth century, America's jazz movement introduced brass instruments and improvisation to the scene. Of Cuba's musical traditions, the *danzón* remains the most influential with its French and African heritage, whereas *son* music is known as the father of the American rumba and its offspring in the States.

Indeed, it was the rumba that emerged at the dawn of the Great Depression as a new musical style introduced to mainstream American audiences by

ABOVE:
Maracas originated with Cuba's native peoples.

ABOVE RIGHT:
Xavier Cugat spread the gospel of Cuban rhythm throughout America.

RIGHT:
Ernesto Lecuona was Cuba's Gershwin, with many U.S. hits.

the ballroom orchestras of New York's big hotels. The man most responsible for spreading the gospel of Cuban rhythm was Xavier Cugat, the Spanish–Cuban bandleader at the helm of New York's Waldorf Astoria Hotel orchestra. Cugat became America's ambassador of Cuban music during the 1930s and 1940s as he traveled with his orchestra to ballrooms throughout the United States. He also regularly performed on radio, appeared in Hollywood movies, recorded dozens of popular Latin-inspired albums, and nurtured new talent. A key component of Cugat's repertoire was the music of Ernesto Lecuona, the "Cuban Gershwin," whose compositions "Malagueña," "Jungle Drums," "Siboney," and "Andalucia (The Breeze and I)" were huge hits.

In the United States, the rumba soon came to mean Cuban-influenced dance music of various genres. The music quickly sparked rumba fever, the first of many Cuban-inspired dance crazes—such as the conga, mambo, and cha-cha-chá—to conquer the United States over the next thirty years. The American version of rumba (or rhumba) became associated with a flashy ballroom dance that differed markedly from the Afro-Cuban rumba, which arose

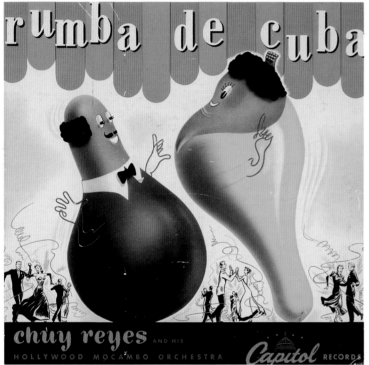

from the island's slums where it was fast, aggressive, and sexually charged.

One of the gifted Cuban musicians to emerge from Xavier Cugat's orchestra in the early 1940s was the singer Miguelito Valdés, who is credited with introducing his conga style to the United States. Valdés's popularity led him to form his own band,

As inimitably featured by
MIGUELITO VALDES

ABOVE:
Conga master Miguelito Valdés was "Mister Babalu" years before Desi Arnaz.

RIGHT:
Tito Puente (second from right) got his start with José Curbelo's orchestra in the 1940s.

and he toured the world as "Mister Babalu" years before Desi Arnaz claimed the title with his recording of the Santería-flavored song in 1946. Another important Cuban musician performing in Manhattan during the 1940s was José Curbelo, whose orchestra included the young percussionist and composer Tito Puente, who went on to record one hundred albums, publish hundreds of original compositions, and

win four Grammy awards, the last in 1990. Puente's unique melding of Cuban music with American jazz created an eclectic new Latin sound that defied categorization and made him a legend.

In 1951, just as conga fever was cooling off, the Cuban bandleader and composer Pérez Prado stormed the United States with a genre of Cuban music called mambo (an adaptation

LIVING STEREO

RCA VICTOR
LSP-1556
Stereo-Orthophonic High Fidelity Recording

"PREZ"
PEREZ PRADO

"MIRACLE SURFACE"
This record contains the revolutionary new antistatic ingredient, 317X, which helps keep the record dust free, helps prevent surface noise, helps insure faithful sound reproduction on LIVING STEREO records.

LEFT:
Mambo King Pérez Prado.

INSET:
Perry Como loved mambo, too.

FACING:
The cha-cha-chá took off in the late 1950s.

of the Cuban *danzón*). Prado's commanding musical style and trademark grunts (he actually says "*¡Dilo!*" or "Say it!") made his performances and recordings standouts among other Latin artists. As the "King of Mambo," Pérez Prado spawned dozens of popular mambo-inspired hits by American singers such as Perry Como's "Papa Loves Mambo" and the playful "Mambo Italiano" by Rosemary Clooney.

At the same time the mambo was sweeping America, Cuban composer and violinist Enrique Jorrín was introducing a style of dance music to Cuban audiences that he named cha-cha-chá. Initially calling the new rhythm "mambo-rumba," Jorrín decided that the name cha-cha-chá was more suitable because it mimicked the sound made by dancers' shoes following the music's beat. In comparison with earlier popular (but difficult) Latin dances, the cha-cha-chá was slower and easier for Americans to attempt on the dance floor. Dozens of cha-cha-chá albums were recorded in the late 1950s before it, too, was supplanted by an entirely new Latin American sound—this time from Brazil—the bossa nova, in 1963.

During the three decades of Cuba's musical conquest of America, Cuba's own music scene was evolving as its radio, recording, and cabaret stars gained huge followings in Havana and throughout Latin America (especially Mexico and Venezuela). Music permeated Havana's streets, wafting from small bars, cafés, restaurants, car radios, houses, and apartment buildings, much of it originating from Cuba's CMQ radio and television broadcasts that featured music recorded at Havana's big nightclubs, showcasing many of the popular performers of the day as well as singing contests where new talent was discovered. For Habaneros who couldn't afford the big nightclubs, it was through the radio that they could vicariously experience the magic of the cabaret. In addition, Panart Records, the country's first record company, founded in 1942 by Ramón S. Sabat, released hundreds of Cuban musical albums: danzónes, guajiras, guarachas, congas, as well as children's songs. Sabat left Cuba in 1964 when his company was expropriated, but he continued to support Cuban music with his Panart Recording Company of New York.

Of all Cuba's legendary performers of the 1950s, it was Beny Moré, "El Barbaro del Ritmo" ("The

Barbarian of Rhythm"), who was the most beloved. After many years of performing throughout Latin America, Beny Moré returned to his native Cuba in 1950, becoming a regular at the Ali Bar roadhouse on the outskirts of central Havana. It was here that Beny was finally embraced by his countrymen, personifying the essence of a Cuban performer—creative, audacious, tender, passionate, with a direct emotional appeal to his audience. Moré was of the people—from a poor rural background—but became a master of all Cuban musical genres. According to music historian Spencer Harrington, "Beny Moré is the greatest singer of popular music Cuba has ever produced. Think Frank Sinatra or Nat 'King' Cole and you'll get an idea of how he's perceived in Cuba, and how he should be regarded elsewhere. . . . Few singers in this hemisphere have consistently matched his interpretive gifts, vocal virtuosity, and comfort with a range of styles." Beny Moré's reputation has not faded since his premature death in Cuba in 1963

at the age of forty-three, with numerous performers celebrating his career in live performances and recordings. Among these, Tito Puente's tribute album *Homenaje a Beny* (Homage to Beny) won a Grammy award in 1979.

Meanwhile, at Havana's hotels, nightclubs, and cabarets catering primarily to tourists, it was performances of the Cuban rumba that were in great demand, complementing the glitzy floorshows and singing stars that formed the centerpiece of a night's entertainment. Famous rumba dance teams such as Clara and Alberto made the rounds at Havana's showrooms, dazzling audiences with their energy and flair.

ABOVE LEFT: Orquesta Vasalo in 1956.

ABOVE RIGHT: Panart was Cuba's first record company.

ABOVE:
Beny Moré was Cuba's
most beloved performer.

RIGHT:
The matchless Beny
Moré.

BENY MORE
EL INIGUALABLE

HIGH FIDELITY
Discuba
LPD-531
ALTA FIDELIDAD

EL INIGUALABLE

One of Cuba's most celebrated cabaret stars in the 1950s was Celia Cruz. Later known as "The Queen of Salsa," Celia Cruz began her career in Havana, singing on the radio and then with Sonora Matancera, a renowned Cuban orchestra. As a solo artist she headlined floorshows at the Tropicana, Sans Souci, and Montmartre nightclubs, integrating her trademark shout *"Azúcar!"* ("Sugar!") into many performances. In 1960, following the Cuban Revolution, Celia Cruz moved to the United States where she performed with her orchestra at major American venues—such as New York City's Palladium Ballroom—until 1965, when she ventured into a solo career. In the ensuing years Cruz recorded with Latin music stars Tito Puente and Johnny Pacheco, eventually joining the ensemble salsa group the Fania All Stars, which led to her fame as the world's Salsa Queen. Following a 1990 Grammy Award for Best Tropical Latin Performance, Celia Cruz appeared in the film *The Mambo Kings,* was awarded the National Medal of Arts by President Bill Clinton in 1994 and, in 2001, recorded her final album. She died two years later, in 2003, at her home in Fort Lee, New Jersey.

Salsa music, for which Celia Cruz was so intimately associated in her later life, is a term used to describe Cuban-derived musical genres as varied as the rumba, mambo, and cha-cha-chá reinterpreted in the late 1960s by Cuban and Puerto Rican emigrants in the New York City area. Salsa, which in Spanish refers to a spicy sauce, quickly spread throughout Latin communities in the United States and the world, gaining increasingly diverse meanings that are difficult to define. Indeed, the terms *Latin jazz, musica tropical,* and *salsa* can be used interchangeably. Although essentially Cuban in stylistic origin, salsa now embraces Puerto Rican and other Latin styles, including pop, jazz, and rock, and is the most popular form of music played at Latin dance clubs.

In recent years there has been a rediscovery of traditional Cuban music due to the efforts of guitarist and producer Ry Cooder with his recordings (and documentary) of the Buena Vista Social Club. The remarkable talents of Ibrahim Ferrer, Compay

Segundo, Rubén González, Eliades Ochoa, Manuel "Puntillita" Licea, Omara Portuondo, and others have found a new international audience, reminding us of the outsized impact that one Caribbean island has had on the world's musical heritage.

Havana. Typical Cuban Rumba.

ABOVE:
Legendary rumba dancers Clara and Alberto.

RIGHT:
The future salsa queen Celia Cruz circa 1954.

Havana and the Mob

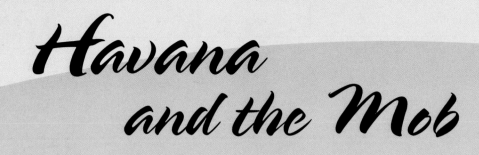

"This is going to be another Las Vegas,"
a promoter boasted, "only like Las
Vegas never imagined."

—*Life*, March 10, 1958

RIGHT:
Meyer Lansky's new Riviera casino.

The influence of the mob in 1950s Havana has been enlarged and exaggerated over the years and was not in itself a major instigator of the revolution. On the contrary, it was the intense hatred of Batista stemming from his 1952 coup d'etat, his quashing of democratic institutions, and the brutality of his army and police that drove the opposition toward the dictator's violent overthrow. Undeniably, though, the big new hotels and swank nightclub casinos became a visible presence of the American mob in Havana after Batista's takeover and were a potent symbol of government corruption and prime targets for revenge when Batista finally fell.

It was in the late 1930s, during Batista's years as Cuba's behind-the-scenes power broker, that the mob made its first appearance in Havana. Mismanagement and outright cheating at Cuba's

Oriental Park Racetrack, home to the Gran Casino Nacional and the small Jockey Club casino, had led American Thoroughbred horse owners and bettors to avoid these once-glamorous attractions. To bring the Americans back, then-Colonel Batista invited the well-respected New England horse- and dog-track operator Lou Smith to reform Oriental Park's operations in 1938. Smith, in turn, brought in Meyer Lansky to clean up the casinos, which Lansky did with alacrity. Although Batista and Lansky had not met prior to that time, Lansky's reputation as a professional gambler who knew how to run a clean casino preceded him. In fact, the Batista–Lansky relationship would reemerge in spectacular fashion fifteen years later when Batista put himself back into power and needed Lansky to perform a similar role in restoring the status of Havana's once again tainted casinos.

Just who was Meyer Lansky and how did he come to be the kingpin of Havana's gambling showcases in the 1950s? Robert Lacey's extraordinary biography *Little Man: Meyer Lansky and the Gangster Life* is the definitive source for information on the life of one of America's most notorious underworld figures. Meyer Lansky was born Meyer Suchowljansky in Russia around 1902. Fleeing the Czarist pogroms, Meyer's father Max departed for America in 1909, sending for his wife and children two years later. They eventually settled in New York's Lower East Side ghetto with their new surname, Lansky, and years of hardship and struggle before them.

By his late teens Meyer Lansky was studious and somewhat introverted, but he was also tough, determined, and strong-willed—and of exceptionally short stature, reaching a height of only five feet three inches as an adult. His Lower East Side upbringing put him in the company of other poor emigrant groups—Irish and Sicilians—where youth gangs and violence were part of daily life. It was in this rough-and-tumble milieu that the teenage Lansky became close friends with Salvatore (Charlie) Lucania (later changed to Luciano), a smart Italian street tough the same age as Lansky, and Benjamin Siegel, a

LEFT:
Havana gambling kingpin
Meyer Lansky in 1958.

good-looking, hotheaded Jewish boy five years Meyer's junior. It was with these two, "Lucky" Luciano and "Bugsy" Siegel, that Meyer Lansky's fate would be intertwined for the next thirty years. And it was in this atmosphere that Lansky was first exposed to small-time gamblers and the realization that he had a natural aptitude for the mathematical probabilities associated with dice games.

During the 1920s it was Prohibition that allowed America's criminal underworld to mature and flourish. In Manhattan, the Lansky brothers, Meyer and Jake, teamed up with with Luciano and Siegel and became successful bootleggers and operators of speakeasies and gambling dens. While each was arrested, mug shots taken, charges filed—and usually dismissed—none of them spent more than a few days in jail throughout the entire decade. By the mid-1930s, through murder and intimidation, Lucky Luciano had secured his place as New York's de facto crime boss. For his part, following the repeal of Prohibition, Meyer Lansky focused on building his reputation as a gambler by organizing floating crap and card games and running one of the big profitable "carpet joints" during the summer gaming seasons in upstate New York's posh Saratoga Springs resort. The term *carpet joint* referred to the plush carpeting, rich furnishings, and first-class floor shows of the illegal lakeside gambling houses built to attract wealthy bettors who came to Saratoga each season to attend Thoroughbred horse racing and soak in the sulfur baths.

Biographer Robert Lacey wrote that Lansky would later reminisce on "a career spent in the rattle, click, and murmur of the gaming room—the green felt, the dark wood, the glamorous, brightly colored chips. He was talking of the players, the men with

their eyes and their hearts fixed on the table, losing themselves, and hoping to find something else in their contest with the dice or card or wheel. But Meyer Lansky could have been talking about himself, for it was in the course of his Saratoga summers that he discovered he was made to run casinos." Lacey continued, "Running a casino is an art form all its own: the ability to conjure up the glamour and escapism that will entice others to wager—the illusion that money is not really money—while retaining your own workaday, bedrock restraint, the ruthless sense of business to make sure that the cash ends up in your pocket. Meyer Lansky had the sense of style, and he also had the discipline."

Lansky had also learned that to attract and keep serious bettors at his gaming tables his casinos must be scrupulously clean—free of any whiff of cheating. Otherwise "a crap game or a casino can be dead in a matter of hours, and once dead, it stays dead. So, as with his bootlegging, Meyer Lansky found himself in an illegal enterprise where enduring success depended on being honest." It was as the impresario of professional gambling that Lansky expanded his operations to southern Florida's city of Hallandale in 1936, which led to his invitation by Lou Smith to clean up Havana's casinos in 1938. Cuba was "Meyer's first experience operating gambling in an open and legal fashion, with no need for protection payments or for quasi-legal subterfuges, and he liked it," reported Lacey.

Back in New York, in contrast with the publicity-shy Lansky, Lucky Luciano had become a big presence in a big city and, as its most prominent gangster, became the prime target of crusading prosecutor Thomas E. Dewey. In 1937, Dewey secured the conviction of Luciano with a thirty-to-fifty-year prison sentence for multiple counts of pandering. Yet nine years later, in 1946, Luciano was set free and deported to Italy due to his assistance—utilizing his labor union and port connections—in helping secure the New York waterfront from enemy sabotage during World War II. After a brief respite in his native Sicily, Luciano surfaced in Havana to preside over the infamous mob summit held at the Hotel Nacional in December 1946, which was attended by the biggest gangsters of the era, including Frank Costello, Albert Anastasia, Joe Bonnano, Vito Genovese, and Joe Adonis of New York and New Jersey; Chicago's Fischetti Brothers; Moe Dalitz and "Doc" Stacher of Cleveland; and Tampa's numbers king Santo Trafficante Jr. Assisting Luciano in the arrangements was his close friend Meyer Lansky. Topping the summit's Christmas week

celebrations was a performance by the young Italian-American crooner Frank Sinatra, of whose success the mob leaders were very proud. It was also at the Havana summit that the Flamingo Hotel and Casino's financial problems in Las Vegas, which had arisen due to the excesses and mismanagement of the flamboyant Bugsy Siegel, were reportedly discussed, ultimately leading to Siegel's murder in Hollywood six months later, over the reputed objections of his old pal Lansky.

Las Vegas, however, never much appealed to Meyer Lansky. He didn't like the desert and was more attracted to the gambling action in southern Florida and, after 1952, Havana, Cuba. In addition, after Lansky was identified as one of America's top crime lords during the United States Senate's Kefauver Crime Committee Hearings of 1950–51, the Nevada Gaming Commission essentially banned Lansky from ever receiving a casino license in that state.

Within just a few months of Batista's 1952 coup, Lansky was back in Havana negotiating a controlling interest in the big well-established Montmartre nightclub/casino located in the city's trendy Vedado district. Lansky's stature on the island ratcheted up substantially when President Batista named him as the government's official advisor on gambling reform following the notorious razzle-dazzle cheating scandal of 1953. As Lacey put it, "Meyer might be an outlaw in America, but in Cuba he was welcomed as the man who knew how to put things straight" because "it was Batista's ambition, with the help of Meyer Lansky, to turn Havana into the Monte Carlo of the Caribbean."

Once Lansky rid Havana of its crooked gamblers and cheats, the sole remaining American mobster

LEFT:
Capo "Lucky" Luciano in Sicily following his deportation from the United States in 1946.

controlling a local casino was Santo Trafficante Jr., who had been in Cuba since the mob summit of 1946. Unlike many high-living, high-profile American gangsters, Trafficante was almost professorial in his crew cut, glasses, conservative suits, and reserved manner. After 1948, when the new administration of Cuban president Carlos Prío Socarrás once again legalized casino gambling, Trafficante Jr. was well positioned to invest heavily in Havana casinos, taking control of the Sans Souci nightclub in suburban Marianao and quickly transforming it into a gambling mecca. In the mid-1950s, Frank "Lefty Clark" Bischoff was brought on to supervise and promote Sans Souci's gaming operations—a role that he would also briefly play at the Tropicana nightclub's casino.

Meyer Lansky's respect for Havana's majestic Hotel Nacional, site of the 1946 mob summit, with its prime location facing the Malecón, led to his orchestration in 1955 of the government-owned property being placed under the management of Pan Am subsidiary Intercontinental Hotels Corporation (IHC). As part of a multimillion-dollar refurbishment, the hotel would inaugurate a new casino to be sublet to a third-party operator—Meyer Lansky and associates. These associates included several old friends from

COLORFUL...

ELEGANT...

WORLD-FAMOUS...

HAVANA, CUBA

HOTEL NACIONAL DE CUBA

AN INTERCONTINENTAL HOTEL

Lansky's bootlegging days—Moe Dalitz and Sam Tucker of the mostly Jewish Cleveland Gang. With brother Jake Lansky as the casino's floor manager, it was left to Wilbur Clark, front man of Las Vegas's Desert Inn, to provide the prestige needed to attract the high rollers. Of the arrangement, Lacey noted, "The Lansky brothers were operating in partnership with a regime which was corrupt. But they did not allow that corruption to touch the purity of what made them real money—serious, professional gambling."

Also in 1955, Batista passed Hotel Law 2074, a bill that had an immediate impact on the mob's Havana operations by offering tax incentives, government loans, and casino licenses to any new hotel with more than $1 million of new investment or any new nightclub valued at $200,000. "Hotel Law 2074 was also the channel by which the president could dispense government money to associates like Meyer Lansky, who then made sure that it was friends and relatives of the president who profited privately from the construction and operation of the new hotel-casinos that they built," wrote Lacey. With

the new law came the great Havana building boom of 1956–1958, when the Hotel Capri, Havana Riviera, and Habana Hilton were constructed and outfitted with the biggest, most extravagant casinos outside of Las Vegas.

First to be erected was the glittering Hotel Capri, a modern nineteen-story edifice with the novelty of a rooftop swimming pool. Although the Capri's casino was fronted by the actor George Raft, who had built his career playing and befriending real-life gangsters (such as Bugsy Siegel), its real owner was Santo Trafficante Jr. Another of Trafficante's casinos was located in the smaller beachfront Hotel Comodoro, situated in Havana's nearby Miramar district.

Next on the drawing board under the terms of Hotel Law 2074 was Meyer Lansky's ultraswank

ABOVE LEFT AND ABOVE:
Wilbur Clark was the mob's front man for Vegas's Desert Inn and Havana's Hotel Nacional.

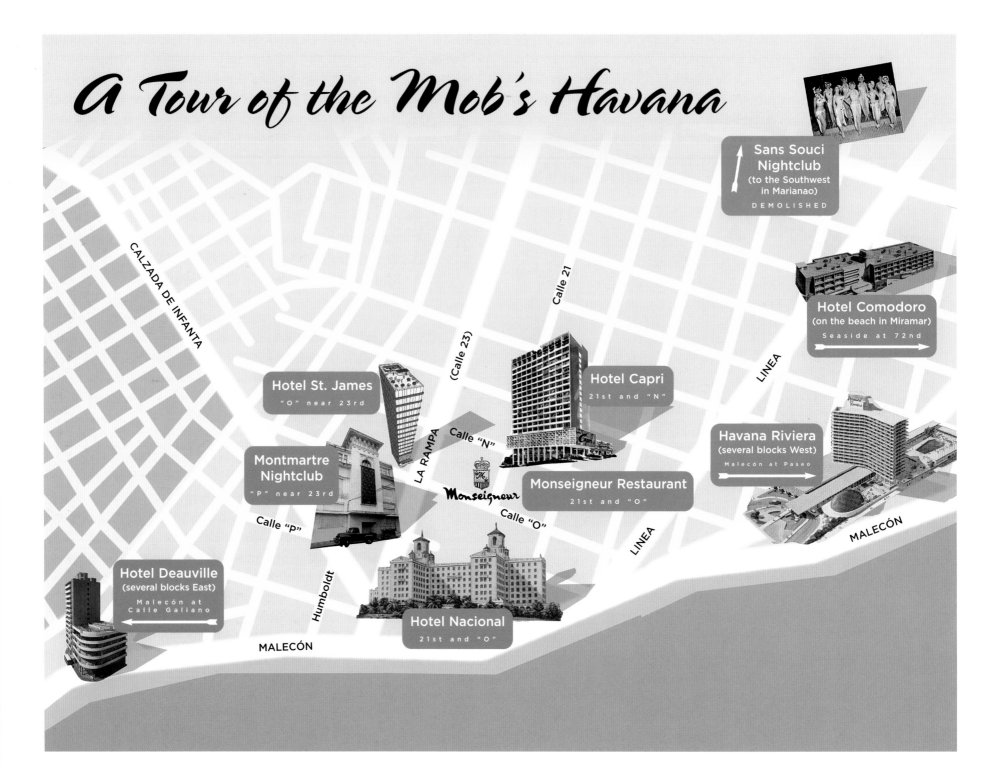

A Tour of the Mob's Havana

Sans Souci Nightclub
(to the Southwest in Marianao)
DEMOLISHED

Hotel Comodoro
(on the beach in Miramar)
Seaside at 72nd

Hotel St. James
"O" near 23rd

Hotel Capri
21st and "N"

Havana Riviera
(several blocks West)
Malecón at Paseo

Montmartre Nightclub
"P" near 23rd

Monseigneur

Monseigneur Restaurant
21st and "O"

Hotel Deauville
(several blocks East)
Malecón at Calle Galiano

Hotel Nacional
21st and "O"

CALZADA DE INFANTA

(Calle 23)

Calle 21

LA RAMPA

Calle "N"

Calle "P"

Calle "O"

Humboldt

LINEA

LINEA

MALECÓN

MALECÓN

Pyramids of Mob Control

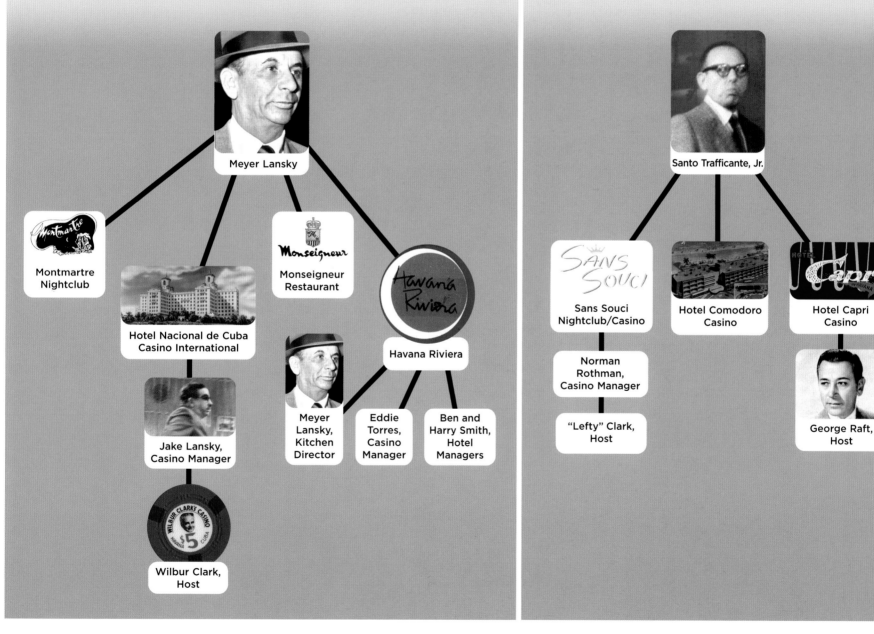

Meyer Lansky

Montmartre Nightclub

Hotel Nacional de Cuba Casino International

Monseigneur Restaurant

Havana Riviera

Jake Lansky, Casino Manager

Meyer Lansky, Kitchen Director

Eddie Torres, Casino Manager

Ben and Harry Smith, Hotel Managers

Wilbur Clark, Host

Santo Trafficante, Jr.

Sans Souci Nightclub/Casino

Hotel Comodoro Casino

Hotel Capri Casino

Norman Rothman, Casino Manager

"Lefty" Clark, Host

George Raft, Host

Havana Riviera

"Havana in the Grand Manner!"

—Havana Riviera slogan, 1957

HAVANA IN THE GRAND MANNER!

Havana Riviera HOTEL / CASINO

VEDADO ON THE MALECON, HAVANA, CUBA

Under the terms of Cuba's Hotel Law 2074 passed in 1955, Meyer Lansky rapidly arranged the financing of his dream project—the Havana Riviera— which would be the most extravagant and sophisticated high-rise resort hotel–casino in the Caribbean, rivaling

ABOVE:
The hotel's slick 1958 brochure.

RIGHT:
Havana Riviera in 2007.

182

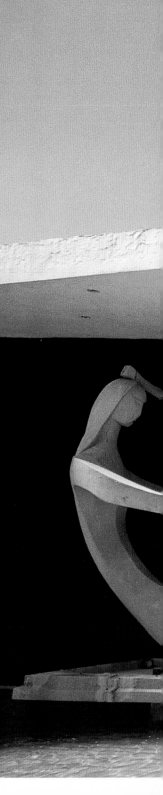

the great pleasure palaces of Miami Beach and Las Vegas. In financing the project, $8 million came from Lansky and his associates; $6 million came from Batista government loans. Lansky's investment partners included some of Las Vegas's biggest power brokers, among them his old friends Moe Dalitz, Morris Kleinman, Sam Tucker, and Wilbur Clark of the Desert Inn (and of Lansky's Hotel Nacional casino); Edward Levinson of the Fremont Hotel; and Hyman Abrams and Morris Rosen of the Flamingo (of Bugsy Siegel fame). As with all of Lansky's dealings, he and his underworld associates' ownership of the Riviera was hidden behind layers of managers and front men.

In selecting an architect for the Havana Riviera, Lansky initially approached Wayne McAllister, who was the prolific Los Angeles–based designer of Las Vegas's stylish Desert Inn, Fremont, and Sands hotels—all properties controlled by Lansky's associates in the "Cleveland Gang." According to historian Chris Nichols as reported in his excellent book *The Leisure Architecture of Wayne McAllister,* Lansky's insistence that the hotel be completed in less than six months led McAllister to respectfully decline the commission. Instead, Igor Polevitzky, one of the deans of Miami Modern architecture, took the job. Irving Feldman served as the project's general contractor.

Russian-born Igor B. Polevitzky (1911–1978) arrived in Miami in 1934 after receiving his architecture degree from the University of Pennsylvania. He, along with a handful of young innovators such as

ABOVE LEFT:
Architect Igor Polevitzky.

ABOVE CENTER:
Polevitzky's seminal Miami Beach Shelborne Hotel of 1940.

ABOVE:
Riviera architectural model.

FACING, RIGHT:
The Riviera's rear elevator core in 2007.

Thomas Triplett Russell (who was Polevitzky's architectural partner from 1936 to 1941), drew inspiration from the Streamline Moderne and International Style in creating a new tropical Modernism that responded to the challenges of the intense sun, wind, and humidity of southern Florida. Of the firm's pre–World War II buildings, the 1940 Shelborne Hotel had the greatest impact on the direction of Miami architecture in the postwar period, influencing Morris Lapidus's Eden Roc and Fontainebleau hotels in its extensive use of plate glass windows, horizontal window bands, and sculptural qualities.

With his new partner Vernon Johnson, Igor Polevitzky approached the Havana Riviera project with gusto and creativity. Situated on a broad stretch of the dramatic seaside Malecón roadway in the city's chic Vedado district, the twenty-one-story hotel tower was designed in a Y configuration, raised on thin columns to take full advantage of magnificent views of the Gulf of Mexico from the guest rooms and the vast lobby area. By extending the floor slabs beyond the exterior walls and scalloping the end of the building's cantilevered ocean-facing wing, the architects gave the design an exciting sculptural quality while providing welcome shade to the guest rooms. Soothing turquoise-colored Italian-glass mosaic tile covers the tower's surfaces (the cost of which Meyer Lansky bitterly complained), linking the building to the adjacent Caribbean Sea. As Havana's first major building with central air conditioning, the Riviera was a cool refuge from the often-sticky tropics.

For the Riviera's interiors, Albert Parvin of the Parvin-Dohrman Company of Los Angeles—the premier decorating firm for Las Vegas's newest resorts—completely furnished the hotel, designing custom pieces for the lobby, restaurants, cocktail lounges, Copa showroom, and guest rooms. Enhancing the Riviera's splendor were unique sculptures, wall pieces, paintings, and murals by some of Cuba's best artists of the 1950s. The renowned sculptor Florencio Gelabert designed two of the

CLOCKWISE, ABOVE:
Albert Parvin of Los Angeles designed the hotel's furnishings. Suite. Lobby as seen in 2007. Guest room.

FACING:
Rolando López Dirube's magnificent abstract mural covers the casino's entry wall in 2007.

hotel's most prominent semiabstract masterpieces: a white marble sculpture of an intertwined mermaid and swordfish that fronts the entrance porte cochere, and *Ritmo Cubano* (*Cuban Rhythm*), a large lobby sculpture that depicts twirling male and female dancers rendered in bronze. An astounding abstract bas-relief mural rendered in plaster, metal wire, and backlit resin, designed by Rolando López Dirube, covers the entire wall surface of the entry hall leading from the lobby to the casino. And centering the lobby's grand circular staircase that descends to the hotel's Primavera Coffee Shop is a spectacular two-story abstract metal sculpture by Cundo Bermúdez.

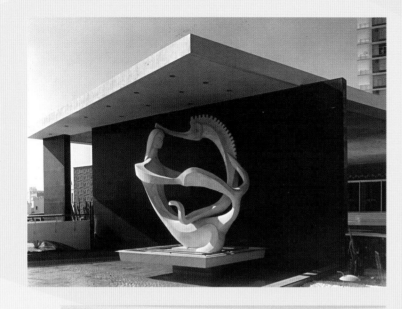

Renowned Cuban sculptors filled the hotel with custom artwork. Florencio Gelabert designed the mermaid and swordfish entrance sculpture (above left) and the lobby's *Ritmo Cubano* (*Cuban Rhythm*, left). A two-story abstract metal sculpture by Cundo Bermúdez (above and right) centers the lobby's circular staircase.

Albert Parvin's dazzling design for the Riviera's L'aiglon Restaurant made "Dining in the Grand Manner" a singular event. Promotional literature boasted that at L'aiglon, "The atmosphere is cosmopolitan; the décor tropical; the service continental; the food superb!" Beneath fantastic crystal chandeliers, guests were surrounded by Regency-style candelabras, gold-veined mirrors, and whimsical murals by artist Hipólito Hidalgo de Caviedes, depicting Cubans celebrating carnival. The exceptional quality of L'aiglon's cuisine was due to Lansky's obsession with serving the finest food, based upon his years of experience in managing upscale "carpet joints" (illegal nightclub–casinos) in New York and Florida. In his official role as the Riviera's kitchen director, a position that Lanksy took quite seriously, he oversaw the menu selection and demanded that only the finest Midwest corn-fed beef be served at L'aiglon.

CLOCKWISE FROM LEFT:
Frozen in time, L'aiglon's interior in 2007.
"Dining in the Grand Manner." L'aiglon in
1958. Sophisticated entertainment. Artist's
rendering in 1957.

ABOVE:
L'aiglon's festive carnival mural by Hipólito Hidalgo de Caviedes as seen in 2007.

the hotel's opening night headliner. Of Miss Rogers' performance, Lansky complained, "She can wiggle her ass but she can't sing a goddamn note."

Magnifying the new hotel's prestige was the live television broadcast of NBC's popular *Steve Allen Show,* beamed to a huge American audience from the Havana Riviera on January 19, 1958. The show opened with Allen on the Copa Room stage,

ABOVE:
Enjoying preshow libations at the Riviera's L'elegante lounge in 1958.

RIGHT:
L'elegante's sparkling metal and colored-glass hanging lamps in 2007.

Given the Riviera's dual role as an entertainment showcase and high-style casino, the entrances to these key venues were to the immediate left and right, respectively, of the hotel's main lobby doors. Beneath an enormous egg-shaped dome lit by custom-designed gold and crystal chandeliers were the casino's table games—roulette, blackjack, craps, *chemin de fer* (baccarat)—with a row of slot machines lining the curved perimeter wall. The sunken "Doble o Nada" ("Double or Nothing") bar off the casino floor was just one of the hotel's three venues providing live entertainment. The fabulous Copa Room (modeled after Vegas's Sands showroom of the same name) was inaugurated on December 10, 1957, when Ginger Rogers was

Riviera glamour in the casino (left), Copa Room (above), the casino's Doble o Nada lounge (far right), and L'elegante lounge (right).

Havana Riviera

2/19/58

quipping, "Here we are in Havana, the home of the pineapple and Meyer Lansky and it's wonderful to be here," followed by comedy routines featuring Lou Costello, Edgar Bergen, and the bug-eyed Don Knotts; a continuous lip-synching musical stroll through the casino, lobby, and outside to the swimming pool by crooner Steve Lawrence; and some poolside cavorting by blonde bombshell Mamie Van Doren. The value to Cuban tourism of Steve Allen's live broadcast was incalculable, as millions of viewers witnessed Americans like themselves packing the

BELOW AND RIGHT:
The Copa Room in 1958. A dazzling Copa Room dinner show.

casino and wandering the lobby, obviously having a grand time in naughty Havana.

In the 1950s, renting a luxury poolside cabana for sunbathing, card playing, and lounging with a cocktail was a popular status symbol, particularly in Miami Beach. The Fontainebleau's enormous serpentine double-decked cabana row (long gone) was probably the most renowned in its day. In Havana, the Hotel Nacional's early-1950s makeover introduced the poolside cabana concept to the city. When Lansky commissioned the Riviera, his Cabana Club included seventy-six individual rooms, one of which was his personal cabana for afternoon games of gin rummy with his cronies.

ABOVE AND RIGHT: The Riviera's pool area as imagined in 1957, and as seen in 2007.

HABANA BILTMORE YACHT AND COUNTRY CLUB

Immediately following the widely acknowledged architectural and financial success of the Havana Riviera, with rooms booked through the 1957–58 winter season, Polevitzky, Johnson & Associates was commissioned by the Habana Biltmore Yacht and Country Club to design an ultramodern replacement for its original 1920s-era facility. What would have been a spectacular tour de force of seductive curves rendered in thin-shell concrete—clearly influenced by Cuban architect Max Borges's Tropicana nightclub and Nautical Club buildings of 1952 and 1953, respectively—was never built when the revolution intervened.

Almost five decades have passed since Castro took the city, yet the Havana Riviera remains virtually unmolested in its original 1957 splendor. Indeed, due to benign neglect, the Riviera is undoubtedly the best-preserved example of midcentury Las Vegas–influenced Miami Modern resort architecture

Havana Riviera Then and Now

ABOVE AND BELOW:
Time travel to 1957 is still possible at the Riviera, the best-preserved midcentury Vegas/Miami Modern resort hotel in the world: exteriors, interiors, fixtures, furnishings, and custom artwork.

in the world. No other hotel of its vintage retains its original high-style exterior architectural elements—including mosaic tile veneer, molded concrete panels, double-deck cabanas, and a three-tiered diving platform—or its interior decor. The original Albert Parvin lobby furnishings (from credenzas to marble coffee tables to low-slung settees that have been merely reupholstered over the years), bronze sculptures and

wall art, pierced screens, terrazzo floors, light fixtures, decorative sconces, door pulls, directional signage, elevator doors, chandeliers, murals, place settings, flatware, dining chairs, and even L'aiglon's original carpeting continue to exist at the Havana Riviera.

Entering the hotel's revolving lobby door magically transports you—without needing to avert your eyes or pretending to ignore historically inappropriate intrusions—back to the height of pre-Castro

glamour as it once existed in the "Monte Carlo of the Caribbean." The period atmosphere that Miami Beach's Eden Roc has attempted to restore and that the Fontainebleau and Americana have sadly lost—not to mention the callous destruction of Las Vegas's Rat Pack–era hotel-casinos—actually survives in its original splendor at the Havana Riviera. For how much longer? Who knows.

Of Meyer Lansky's commitment to Havana in 1958, his biographer Robert Lacey concluded, "Meyer had staked his personal bankroll solidly on the success of the Riviera—to the exclusion of almost everything else. His spectacular hotel-casino was to be the culmination—and ultimate vindication—of his career. Meyer Lansky might never be able to operate openly in Las Vegas, or anywhere else in America. But here, standing tall, and glinting magnificently over the straits of Florida, was his Xanadu, grand, profitable, and legal. . . . Meyer Lansky invested much more than his money in the Havana Riviera. He invested himself."

ABOVE:
Astonishingly, even the L'aiglon's china and flatware are from 1957.

RIGHT:
A contemporary view of the casual Al Fresco terrace cafe that looks out onto the pool and the sea.

Habana Hilton

"Latin America's Tallest, Largest Hotel!"

—Habana Hilton slogan, 1958

Strikingly Modern, sited at the crest of La Rampa (Twenty-Third Street)—the gently sloping boulevard that rises from the seaside Malecón to the vibrant heart of 1950s Havana—the Habana Hilton stands as vivid testimony to the brief moment when dictator Fulgencio Batista's vision of the city as Latin America's premier tourist destination was fulfilled. Renamed the Habana Libre (Free Habana) after the revolution, the 30-story, 630-room hotel served as Castro's provisional headquarters when he took Havana in January 1959. In many ways, the story of the Habana Hilton encapsulates the final three years of Batista's reign

LEFT:
The Habana Hilton's subtle statement of its stature in Batista's Cuba.

RIGHT:
The renamed Yara Theatre and Habana Libre at dusk in 2007.

when a paroxysm of frenzied hotel and casino construction culminated in the completion—and subsequent confiscation—of the most prominent symbol of American influence in Cuba.

Unlike Lansky's Riviera or Trafficante's Capri, the Habana Hilton was to be primarily a Cuban project with an American face. President Batista was personally involved in shepherding a large government loan in concert with the powerful Catering Workers Union pension fund, which was the project's primary investor and official owner. On account of its unrivaled reputation in attracting North American

tourists to its properties, the union invited Hilton Hotels International (HHI) to coordinate the design and manage the hotel. Stated HHI of the relationship, "The new hotel is unique in the history of private enterprise in that labor and capital have joined hands in the financing and operation of the Habana Hilton. The employers, Hilton Hotels International, as operators of the hotel, will, in effect, be working for their employees."

In early 1956, Hilton chose the premier Los Angeles–based architectural firm of Welton Becket & Associates to design the hotel, with the Frederick

WELTON BECKET & ASSOCIATES
Architects & Engineers
5657 Wilshire Boulevard
Los Angeles 36
WEbster 1-1181

RELEASE: Sunday, March 23, 1958

● The largest and tallest building in Latin America was formally opened in Havana, Cuba, yesterday (Saturday, March 22) when the Hilton Hotels International flag went up atop the Habana Hilton.

Welton Becket, head of the Los Angeles architectural firm that designed the 30-story hotel, and Conrad N. Hilton, president of Hilton Hotels International, welcomed an international assembly of governmental, labor, and industrial leaders, as well as entertainment stars and members of the press to the opening ceremonies.

The 630-room Habana Hilton, built at a cost of $24 million, is the 32nd hotel to carry the Hilton flag. Ceremonies for the dedication included receptions, dinners, balls, Cuban fiestas, sailboat regattas, and other specially-staged entertainment throughout the city.

The hotel will be operated by Hilton Hotels International for its owners, the Caja de Retiro Social de los Trabajadores Gastronomicos (the Catering Workers' Union), whose retirement fund financed the program.

The new hotel is unique in the history of private enterprise in that labor and capital have joined hands in the financing and operation of the Habana Hilton. The employers, Hilton Hotels

—more—

Snare Corporation serving as general contractor. Local Cuban architects Nicolas Arroyo and Gabriela Menendez would collaborate with the Becket team. HHI was quite familiar with the Becket firm's work, having celebrated the opening of the spectacular Beverly Hilton in Beverly Hills, California—a triumph of Becket's "Total Design" philosophy—one year earlier. Welton Becket & Associates had already completed the landmark Capitol Records headquarters building in Hollywood, famous for its round shape

and tall spire, in 1954. In 1963, also in Hollywood, the firm would build the remarkable Cineramadome, the world's only geodesic dome constructed entirely of concrete.

Under Welton Becket's Total Design approach, every aspect of the project—from engineering and architecture to custom furnishings and site-specific artwork—was a product of specialists within the firm. As a result, a consistency of design, execution, and quality could be achieved. In that spirit, Welton Becket himself designed the Habana Hilton's logo based upon the old Havana coat of arms featuring

the three original castles that defended the city: El Morro, La Real Fuerza, and La Punta.

Numerous conceptual drawings were produced in the project's initial stages, with some of the most compelling drawn by the hand of Lee Linton, a designer known for the wildly original, futuristic, Googie-style California coffee shop watercolor renderings he created for Los Angeles's Armet & Davis architectural firm in the mid-1950s. Artist Allan Edwards produced the renderings depicting the hotel's final designs.

Heading up Becket's architectural design team

LEFT TO RIGHT:
Another Lee Linton view. A very different approach to the design. Nearing the final working model.

was Richard Dorman. In charge of interior design was James McQuaid, who arrived in Havana in April 1956 and worked on the project nonstop for two years. In coordination with Hilton's interior design staff, McQuaid was responsible for selecting and managing all of the dozens of manufacturers, artists, and craftspeople involved in creating a unique look that captured the tropical atmosphere of Cuba and the spirit of "old and new Havana."

According to the project's union owners, only Cuban manufacturers could furnish the hotel. Imported materials were allowed only when no Cuban sources were available. Based on McQuaid's designs, the hotel's Cuban-produced furnishings utilized choice local materials such as native hardwoods, rattan, and printed fabrics. Locally sourced coral and volcanic stone appeared as decorative cladding on many of the building's interior and exterior surfaces.

Most of the Habana Hilton's public areas were given a distinctively Cuban theme: the lobby, fashioned

RIOR COURTYARD · PROPOSED HILTON HABANA. CUBA

CLOCKWISE FROM ABOVE LEFT:
The hotel's space-age coffee shop. Unrealized interior courtyard by Lee Linton. Allan Edwards's vision of the El Caribe Supper Club. Deluxe studio room. Typical studio room. Edwards's concept for the casino.

CLOCKWISE FROM FACING:
Caribe Suite living room furnishings designed by James McQuaid, rug by Servando Cabrera Moreno. Castellana Suite master bedroom. Castellana Suite dining room with McQuaid-designed high-backed chairs. Rendering of typical double bedroom.

after a colonial Cuban courtyard with fountains, plants, and statuary; the rooftop Sugar Bar with its chandeliers, chair backs, murals, and wallpaper inspired by the country's sugarcane industry; the Antilles Bar with its ceramic mural wall depicting a Caribbean legend by Cuban artist René Portocarrero. Of the many talented Cuban artists who contributed to the Habana Hilton, it was Amelia Peláez's enormous black, blue, and white mosaic tile mural inspired by the fruits and flowers of Cuba, covering the hotel's primary facade, that transformed the building from a mere hotel to an artistic tour de force. Complementing Peláez's mural was the turquoise Italian-glass mosaic tile used to cover the hotel tower's primary elevations.

While HHI strived to imbue their hotel properties with local flavor, a key component in Hilton's worldwide program was the inclusion of a branch of the swank Trader Vic's Polynesian bar and restaurant chain in its hotels despite (or, perhaps, in celebration

FACING: Sugar Bar Terrace on the twenty-ninth floor.

LEFT: Antilles Bar features a stunning ceramic tile mural by René Portocarrero (see page 250).

UPPER RIGHT: Main lobby patterned after a Cuban interior courtyard.

ABOVE: Main lobby as realized.

of) the cultural incongruity. Thus, at Habana Hilton's Trader Vic's, guests could toast a successful day of touring with either mojitos or mai tais.

A key element in the Habana Hilton's program was its casino. Although it was assumed that Lansky's blessing was required to receive a casino license, he apparently had no say in the Hilton decision. With the backing of Batista and the Culinary Workers Union, the hotel's casino license was sold by Hilton for $1 million to Robert "Chiri" Mendoza, who was from an old and respected Cuban family who owned one of Havana's leading baseball teams. Nonetheless, a storm of unfortunate publicity erupted in January

FACING, FAR LEFT:
The hotel in 1958.

FACING, LEFT:
Entrance area in 2007. It took sixteen million pieces of Italian mosaic tile to create Amelia Peláez's mural of Cuban fruits and flowers.

RIGHT:
Swimming pool terrace in 1958.

Trader Vic's

The concept of creating an urban tropical hideaway in which to drink and dine was inaugurated and brought to perfection by one Don the Beachcomber in the early 1930s. Having visited Don's Hollywood haunt as a sort of "industrial spy," Victor Bergeron took Don's cues and created his own version of Polynesia Americana in Northern California just a few years later, calling it "Trader Vic's." To educate himself further in cocktail mixology, Vic traveled to New Orleans, to Florida, and also to Havana where he learned the recipe for the daiquiri from Constantino Ribalaigua, headman at the La Florida Bar.

Many years later in 1957, when "Trader Vic" Bergeron was asked by Conrad Hilton to build another Trader Vic's at his new Hilton Hotel in Havana, the Trader was not too keen on the idea.

CLOCKWISE FROM BOTTOM LEFT:
Trader Vic Bergeron's sense of humor in 1963. Havana Trader Vic's in 2007. The renamed Polinesio entrance. Trader Vic's 1957 rendering. The same Chinese ovens in 2007.

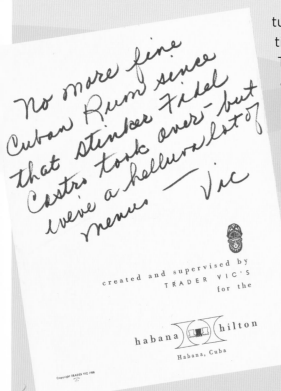

No more fine Cuban Rum since that stinker Fidel Castro took over—but we've a helluva lot of menus — Vic

created and supervised by
TRADER VIC'S
for the

habana **hilton**

Habana, Cuba

Copyright TRADER VIC'S 1988

Granted, Vic's first turnkey franchise operation had been his 1955 Trader Vic's restaurant at the Beverly Hilton in Beverly Hills, and it was doing well. But the Trader knew from experience that Hispanics did not seem to appreciate his restaurant's Polynesian/Chinese fare. Yet, trusting in the tourist market and not wanting to turn Hilton down, he went ahead and built what turned out to be his shortest-lived satellite ever.

Vic's architect was Lloyd Lovegren, who had designed his Chicago and New York Plaza locations in the trademark South Seas Trader style. Scoffing at the conventional American businessmen's attitude that Cuban labor should come cheap, Bergeron felt compelled to pitch in with his local crew's paychecks, which resulted in the restaurant getting finished ahead of schedule before the hotel was completed. This, of course, did not prevent the loss of his business soon after the revolution.

Since then, the Havana Trader Vic's has slept in a Cinderella slumber as the "Polinesio," remaining as one of the best-preserved examples of the style. Ironically, its concept and artifacts served as décor for the Cuban/Russian propaganda film *I Am Cuba* in 1964. In a further twist of art history, the film's nightclub scene, meant to condemn capitalist decadence, is a cineaste's masterwork, which today stands as the best filmic depiction of modernist Pop primitivism.

—Sven A. Kirsten

Starboard Light

In the mid-1950s, Victor Jules "Trader Vic" Bergeron was a tiki empire-builder, with wildly popular Trader Vic's restaurants in major cities across the United States. But like other emperors, he would become most famous not for all the cities he conquered but for the one battle he lost. Vic met his Waterloo in Havana, where in 1958 he built a luxurious Polynesian palace inside the Habana Hilton Hotel. Castro's revolution came soon after the Havana Vic's opened. This drink, the Starboard Light, was one of the "exotics" served at the Havana Vic's before the lights went out. Vic revealed the top-secret recipe in his 1968 book, *Trader Vic's Bartender's Guide*.

—Jeff Berry

Starboard Light

2 teaspoons honey
1 ounce fresh lemon juice
1/2 ounce passion fruit syrup
1 egg white
2 ounces scotch
1 scoop crushed ice

Put everything in a blender and blend at high speed for at least ten seconds. Pour into a Starboard Light glass (pictured). Garnish with fresh mint and a pineapple stick.

1958 when mobster Albert Anastasia's murder in New York was initially tied to his rumored attempt to muscle in on the Habana Hilton's casino operation (a charge that the Hilton people vigorously denied and was never proved). Additionally, throughout the hotel's construction, the constant threat of sabotage hung over the project site like the sword of Damocles as periodic bombings occurred throughout the city in 1957 and 1958.

Yet, somehow, the Habana Hilton's March 22, 1958, grand opening gala occurred without incident, perhaps due to the presence of conspicuously armed policemen guarding the hotel's entrances, the dozens of undercover security officers hired by HHI circulating among the well-dressed guests, and the personal bodyguards accompanying Conrad Hilton and the daughter of United States chief justice Earl Warren, among other celebrities and high-powered guests. The hotel's dazzling Saturday night ball capped a week of receptions, dinners, Cuban fiestas, sailboat regattas, and other special dedication ceremonies staged throughout the city.

Conspicuous at the festivities by his absence was President Fulgencio Batista, who sent his wife Marta to represent the government at the opening ceremonies. Yet everyone knew that the dictator considered the Habana Hilton among his proudest achievements, its huge blue-lit rooftop "Hilton" name announcing to the world that the eminent Conrad N. Hilton had confidence in Cuba's future—that the country was a safe place in which to invest—and that tourists could now find in Havana the modern comforts that they expected in a top international resort.

LEFT:
Welton Becket, Conrad Hilton, and guest of honor Virginia Warren at the grand-opening gala.

FACING:
The Hilton name dominates Havana's skyline in 1958.

Havana's Other Fabulous Hotels

FACING:
The Capri's colorful rendering envisioned the hotel in a luxuriant garden setting instead of its actual location in Havana's urban core.

In addition to the Riviera and Hilton, the fourteen years between the end of World War II and the revolution saw numerous ultramodern Havana hotels erected in response to the tourist boom.

Twenty-First streets, the only place to locate the hotel's swimming pool was on the roof, which the Capri dubbed its "Cabana in the Sky." Fully capturing the drama of the rooftop pool area was the 1964 Russian–Cuban propaganda film *I Am Cuba,* which opens with a long uninterrupted scene featuring decadent Americans ogling competing numbered bathing beauties while lounging over cocktails and card games.

CLOCKWISE FROM LEFT:
A quiet moment on the corner of 21st and N. The Capri in 2007. Diva Celeste Mendoza (facing), "The Queen of the Guaguancó," wows them at the Capri's cabaret in 1958. "Skippy's Hideaway," the Capri's intimate rendezvous lounge (above).

Hotel Nacional de Cuba

"The finest hotel in the Tropics"

— Brochure, 1949

Commissioned during the dictatorship of President Gerardo Machado, the monumental Hotel Nacional de Cuba opened in 1930 on a broad thirteen-acre promontory above the Malecón facing the sea. Having reigned as Cuba's top hostelry for over a quarter century, the Nacional was finally overshadowed by the inauguration of the Havana Riviera in 1957 and the Habana Hilton in 1958.

Designed by one of America's top architectural firms of the period—McKim, Mead and White—the Moorish/Spanish-inspired Nacional became Meyer Lansky's de facto headquarters where, most afternoons, he appeared poolside with his cronies to play gin rummy prior to the opening of his Riviera hotel.

Under Lansky's guidance, Pan Am's Intercontinental Hotel Corporation (IHC) took on the refurbishment and management of the Nacional in 1955. Floor manager of its new Casino International, which Lansky and his associates had licensed, was Meyer's brother Jake—but its front man was Wilbur Clark of Las Vegas's Desert Inn.

LEFT TO RIGHT: The Nacional as seen from the seaside Malecón in 1955 (the USS *Maine* Memorial is on the left). La Sirena (The Mermaid) Bar swizzle. Wilbur Clark's Casino at the Nacional in 1958 (facing).

CLOCKWISE FROM TOP LEFT:
Swimming at the Cabana Club. Hotel Nacional in 2007. Luggage label. "The Cabana Sun Club . . . smart rendezvous of Havana society and cosmopolites for day-long lazing under the Cuban Sun."

HOTEL NACIONAL DE CUBA
ON HABANA'S OCEAN FRONT

Hotel Comodoro

"The Comodoro Hotel . . . in the city . . . by the sea"

—Brochure, 1954

Like Lansky, Tampa-based mobster Santo Trafficante Jr. had interests in a number of Havana casinos, including those at the Sans Souci and Hotel Capri. Another casino licensed to Trafficante was in the Hotel Comodoro, situated on the Atlantic in the nearby Havana suburb of Miramar. Designed in the Late Moderne architectural style with bezeled window bands, a curved elevator tower, and a kidney-shaped entrance canopy, the Comodoro would have fit comfortably in south Miami Beach.

LEFT:
The Miami Modern-style Hotel Comodoro in 2007.

RIGHT:
1954 Comodoro brochure.

hotel *Comodoro*

BY THE SEA AT 72nd AVENUE, MIRAMAR,
HAVANA-CUBA

Other Hotels

Inspired by the Hotel Capri, rooftop swimming pools appeared at the new Hotel Deauville along the Malecón and the "Swim in the Sky" St. Johns, both of which contained modest casinos. The St. Johns was one of three midrange hotels built on O Street near La Rampa (Twenty-Third Street)—the heart of the city's fashionable Vedado district—close to the Montmartre Nightclub and the Hotel Nacional. The other two O Street hotels were the Vedado and Flamingo. The International Style Hotel Lido was built one block west of the Prado promenade. And on the way to the Comodoro in seaside Miramar, one found the brand-new Miami Modern-styled Hotel Copacabana with its own "colorful Cabana Club."

Those desiring a complete escape from busy Havana could take a two-and-a-half-hour drive east to Matanzas province and the "Rhapsody in Blue" waters of Varadero beach. Having selected a prime spot along the narrow sandy peninsula, American hotelier William Liebow commissioned his Hotel Varadero Internacional, which opened in 1950. Liebow added a casino to the property in 1956. Designed in the popular Late Moderne architectural style, the sprawling property remained Varadero's best resort until the 1990s building boom.

Hotel Deauville

With its dramatic location along the seaside Malecón, the Deauville sported a small casino and rooftop swimming pool with cabanas.

Hotel Lido

Located near Central Havana's Prado promenade was the International Style Hotel Lido.

JUST OPENED

Hotel LiDO

CONSULADO 216-218
PHONE W-3964
Havana, Cuba

SAM-ZEILIC MANAGER

Located in the heart of Havana THE LIDO HOTEL is conveniently situated for the shopping center, theatres, Central Park, American Club and the famous Prado Boulevard

"Swim in the Sky" in the Skylark Pool on the roof top, 15 stories high! Relax at the adjacent Skyline Bar and open-air Terrace.

Sunny exuberant days, starry romantic nights are yours to partake of, yours to revel in . . . with your home base the most modern in all Havana . . . the St. Johns. This is not a hotel such as you may have lodged in before, but rather one you may have dreamed of for that special visit. For here, at your command, are the comforts that join with the pleasures of your stay in exotic, exciting Havana.

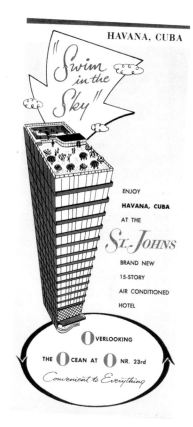

HAVANA, CUBA

"Swim in the Sky"

ENJOY
HAVANA, CUBA
AT THE
St. Johns
BRAND NEW
15-STORY
AIR CONDITIONED
HOTEL

OVERLOOKING
THE OCEAN AT O NR. 23rd

Convenient to Everything

St. Johns

The towering "Swim in the Sky" St. Johns was near the excitement of Vedado's La Rampa entertainment district.

Hotel **Copacabana** AT **HAVANA**

Hotel Copacabana

One of the new seaside resorts modeled after those in the Sunny Isles district of North Miami Beach.

Hotel Vedado

CLOCKWISE FROM RIGHT:
Hotel Vedado in 2007. The hotel's colorful lobby, "a haven of relaxation between activities." Brochure circa 1956. The Vedado Cocktail Lounge, "where strangers become friends."

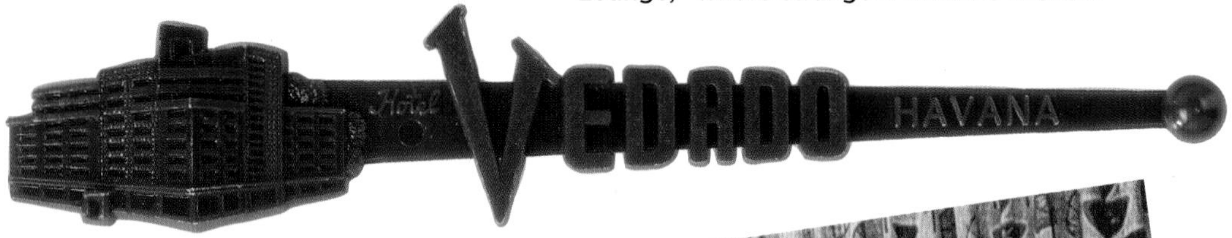
Hotel
VEDADO
HAVANA

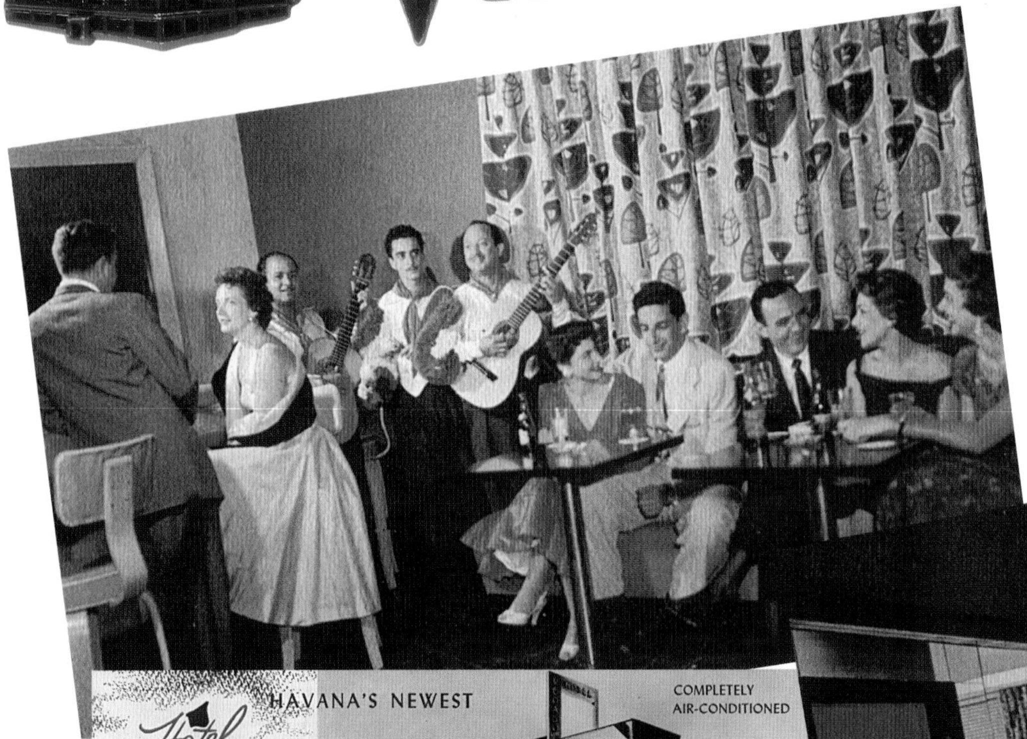

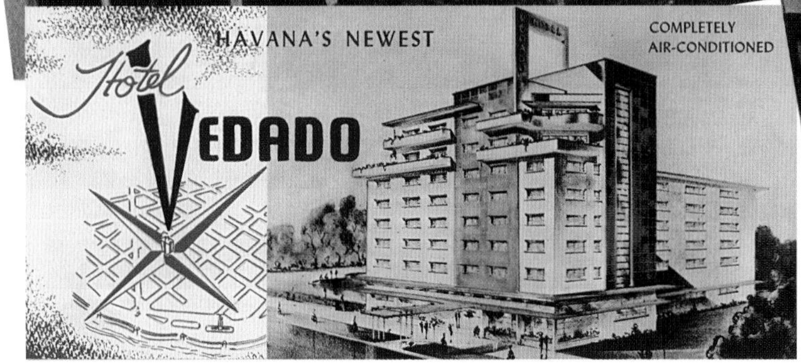
HAVANA'S NEWEST
COMPLETELY AIR-CONDITIONED
Hotel
VEDADO

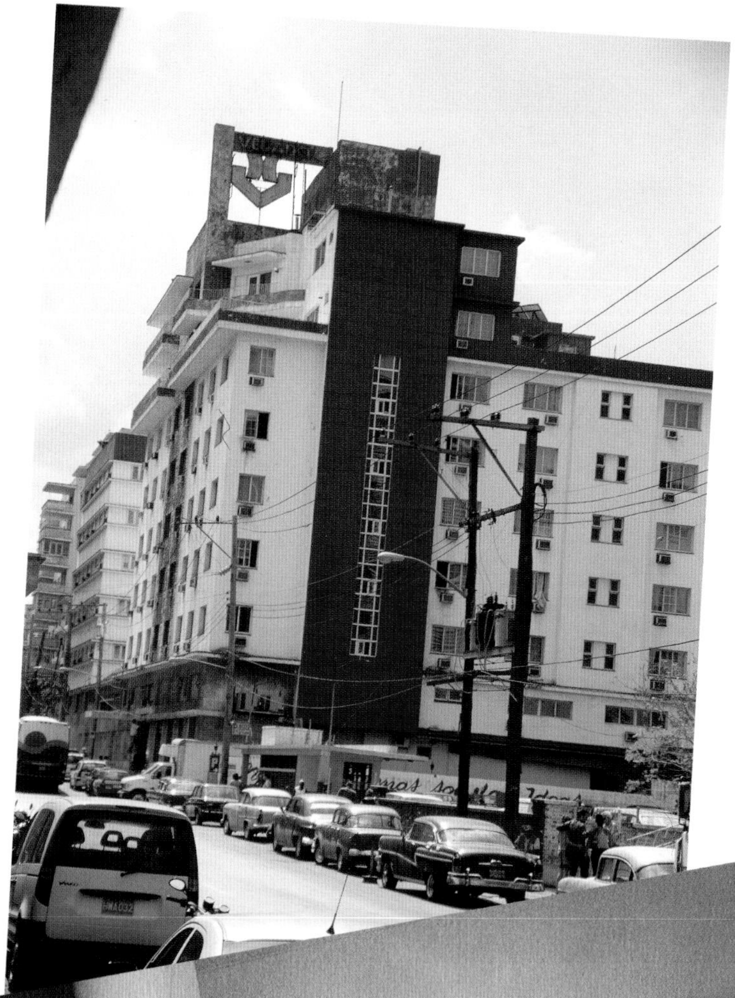

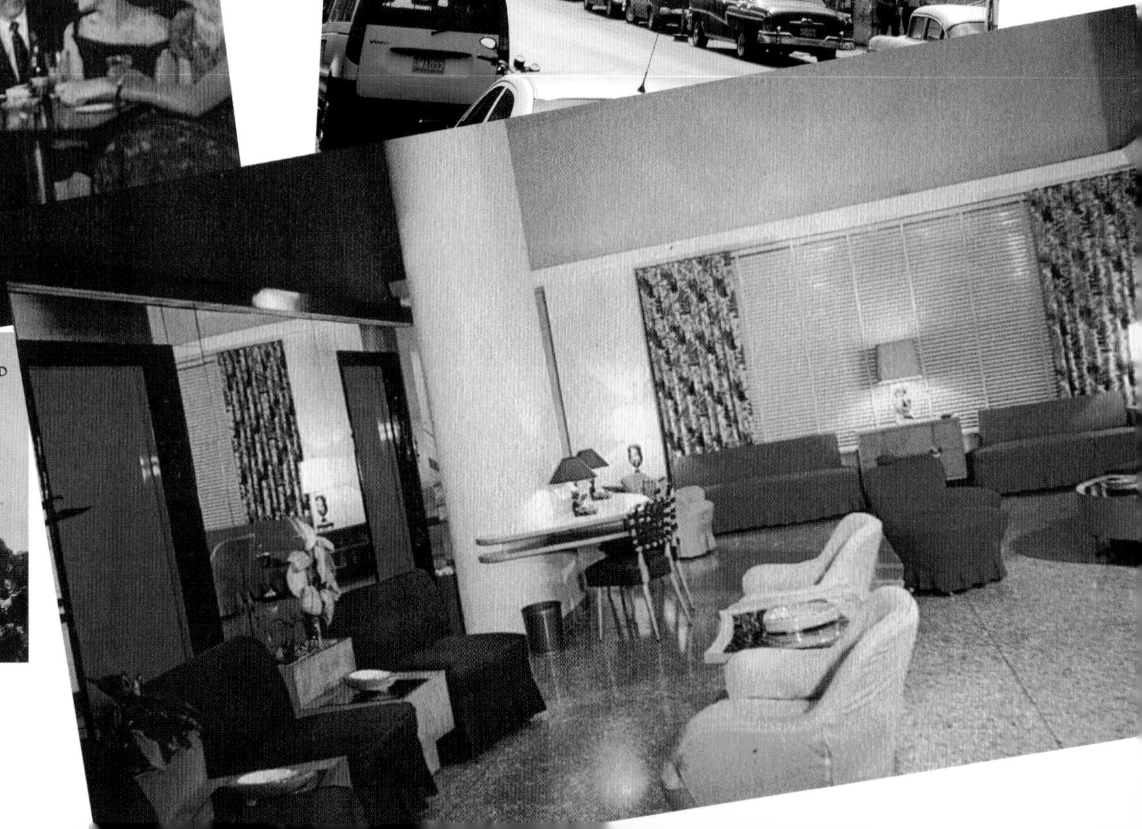

Hotel Varadero Internacional

William Liebow's deluxe Late Moderne-style resort along Cuba's most desirable beach, a few hours east of Havana.

Havana Modern

"[Havana's Modern architecture is] undeniably striking and original, defined by a sinuous, sensual, exhibitionist nonchalance, conveyed by the prodigal use of curves, slender inclined columns, concrete roofs pierced by vegetation and broad cantilevered eaves."

—Eduardo Luis Rodríguez, *The Havana Guide: Modern Architecture 1925–1965*

With all the attention justly being paid to Havana's extraordinary collection of colonial buildings located in La Habana Vieja (Old Havana), symbolized by the district's designation as a UNESCO World Heritage Site in 1982, it is unfortunate that the city's remarkable twentieth-century architectural legacy—particularly its astounding inventory of Modern architecture—remains largely ignored and unpublicized by Cuba's tourist industry. This despite the valiant pioneering efforts of Cuban architectural historian, author, and critic Eduardo Luis

ABOVE:
The Art Deco–style Bacardi Building, 1930.

RIGHT:
Space-age Jibacoa Beach cottages, 1957.

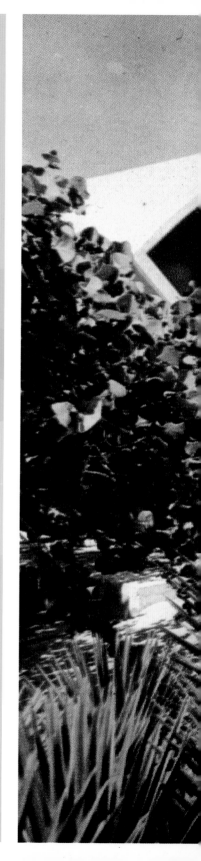

Rodríguez in spearheading the rediscovery and appreciation of Havana's twentieth-century built environment in recent years, particularly its Modern architecture. Of Rodríguez's published work it's his seminal *Havana Guide: Modern Architecture 1925–1965* that remains the only comprehensive tour book of Modern Havana.

Cuba's cornucopia of architectural styles traces its flowering to the nation's independence in 1902 when Spanish colonial influences gave way for the next quarter century to an eclectic melding of neo-classical and Mediterranean Revival styles—whether Spanish, French, or Italian—and a brief early flirtation with the floral Art Nouveau style. During these decades the country experienced several economic booms tied to the price of sugar—Cuba's primary export—that led to the construction of prominent revival-style villas for Havana's newly rich elite, particularly in suburban Vedado but also in the emerging upscale Miramar, Marianao, and Country Club Park districts of the city.

Just as the 1920s economic boom was beginning to fade near decade's end, Art Deco influences appeared in Havana's multistory apartment buildings, downtown storefronts, theatres, and other structures. Like its revival-style precursors, Art Deco

ABOVE: Art Deco-style apartments in Central Havana.

RIGHT: Aqua-colored glazed terra-cotta clads this incredible 1930's retail store.

FAR RIGHT: Remodeling ground-floor retail space at Aguila and San José streets in 1947.

CLOCKWISE
FROM LEFT:
Fausto Theatre in 2007.
Streamlined Moorish-style
residence in 2007. House in
Vedado circa 1935. Solimar
apartments in 1944.
Radiocentro restaurant
circa 1947.

utilized sumptuous building materials such as marble, glazed terra-cotta tile, stained glass, polished
brass and bronze, and colorful terrazzo. But it
departed from the past in emphasizing verticality in
its exterior styling with striations, narrow towerlike
bays, and elongated windows and entrance open-
ings, and zigzag and fountain patterns often con-
trasted with smooth surfaces.

Yet, only ten years later, the Art Deco style was
supplanted by the Streamline Moderne and its
sibling, the Late Moderne. Recognizable by its
emphasis on horizontality, curved corners, round
windows, flat roofs, elongated bands of windows,
stucco sheathing, horizontal striations, and an
absence of applied ornamentation, the Streamline
Moderne style was based upon then-modern modes

of transportation—automobiles, locomotives, passenger ships, airplanes—that were being designed aerodynamically for greater speed and efficiency. In fact, nautical references such as pipe railings, portholes, and roof decks often appeared in Streamline Moderne residential designs.

By the early 1940s an undeniable influence on Cuban architecture came from across the Florida Straits with the phenomenal explosion of new construction in Miami Beach. Between 1940 and 1955, America's most popular winter resort witnessed a proliferation of two- and three-story apartment/hotels, multistory hotel towers, and commercial buildings designed in a Late Moderne architectural style that took the horizontality, streamlining, curved corners, glass blocks, flat roofs, and smooth surfaces of the Streamline Moderne and added prominent bezels to window bands and projecting curved entrance canopies (either cantilevered or supported by slender steel posts) in creating a new Miami Modernism (now known as MiMo). In Havana, the Late Moderne was transitional, paving the way for a distinctly Cuban interpretation of the International Style of architec-

ture in the 1950s up through the 1959 revolution.

The International Style—named for its rejection of historical design precedents in favor of a new, contemporary, non-country-specific (hence, international) approach to architecture—arose out of the 1920s avant-garde Modern Movement based primarily in Germany, whose adherents were forced to flee when the Nazis came to power in the 1930s. Influenced by the movement's most visible proponents—Le Corbusier, Walter Gropius, Ludwig Mies van der Rohe, Richard Neutra, and others—a new generation of Cuban architects, many trained in the United States, began applying European Modernism's International Style tenets to the unique history, culture, setting, and climate of their island nation in creating a new Cuban Modernism.

That the conditions for an exploration of *lo cubano*, or Cuban-ness, in architectural design existed at all was due in large measure to Cuba's

LEFT:
Hotels such as the 1948 Saxony in Miami Beach influenced Havana's postwar Modernism.

BELOW:
Havana Modern goes suburban.

FACING, ABOVE:
Glass walls bring the outdoors in at the 1952 Gastón residence.

FACING, BELOW:
The Noval House of 1949 is raised for air circulation and views.

growing economy as evidenced by its visibly prosperous middle and upper classes—often the necessary precursor to the appearance of cutting-edge architecture in a city. In 1950s Havana, the confluence of a surging tourist industry, increasing agricultural exports, and government-sponsored construction projects led to a flood of commissions for local architects for a tremendous variety of buildings in the city and its environs.

In fashioning a Modernism with a Cuban flair, the integration of certain traditional architectural elements related to the island's tropical climate was essential—outdoor patios, jalousie (louvered) windows for interior air circulation, deep overhanging eaves to shade windows from the bright sun and for protection from the rain, brise soleil (horizontal or vertical exterior sun shades of metal, wood, or concrete that could be fixed or movable), and often interior courtyards. In addition, by raising a residence on stilts, air could circulate beneath it. One of the best early examples of this approach is the José Noval Cueto House by Mario Romañach (of Bosch and Romañach), erected in 1949.

Of the many talented Cuban architects practicing in Havana in the 1950s, it was Max Borges Jr. whose experiments with thin-shell concrete resulted in some of the most compelling Modern buildings erected in Latin America. His Arcos de Cristal (Crystal Arches) of 1951 for the Tropicana nightclub was immediately acclaimed for creating a magical, glittering, and utterly unique space for Cuba's top entertainment venue. Much of the building's success was due to Borges's clever integration of the site's tropical vegetation both inside the space and outside through window bands sandwiched between each of its five telescopic arches. The

design was so successful that the esteemed architectural historian and critic Henry Russell Hitchcock featured it in *Latin American Architecture Since 1945,* an important compendium of Modern architecture published by New York's Museum of Modern Art in 1955.

Two years later, Borges completed the stunning Nautical Club that was also based upon a telescopic arch design—this time with sea waves as inspiration. In creating these masterpieces, Borges consulted with Spanish-Mexican architect Félix Candela, whose expressive thin-shell concrete designs in Mexico were revolutionizing architecture throughout Latin America after World War II.

Through frequent travel, architectural journals, and conferences, Cuban architects kept abreast of the latest engineering and design innovations worldwide. One of the great sources for inspiration was Brazil, where Oscar Niemeyer was transforming the

CLOCKWISE FROM ABOVE:
Max Borges Jr.'s mastery of thin-shell concrete is evident in the curved forms of his buildings. Tropicana, 1951. Nautical Club, 1953. Núñez-Gálvez Tomb, 1957, with Enrique Borges, in 2007 and 1957.

curves of Rio de Janeiro's mountains (and the curves of its women) into an organic architecture utilizing the plasticity of concrete in creating buildings of thrilling sculptural beauty. This new Brazilian Modernism reached its apex in 1960 with the construction of Brasilia, an astonishing utopian vision made manifest. In Havana, the Eugenio Leal Residence (now a restaurant) in seaside Miramar is a superb example of the Cuban approach to Brazilian Modernism.

After the Cuban revolution, most of Cuba's practicing architects departed to the United States, Mexico, Puerto Rico, Spain, France, and elsewhere. Yet their architectural achievements remain—much of them remarkably original—awaiting the embrace of Habaneros and tourists alike who have yet to focus on the totality of the island's architectural heritage instead of just its colonial past.

ABOVE:
Brazilian Modernism at the 1957 Eugenio Leal residence in 2007.

RIGHT:
Sinuous curves and a mosaic tile mural grace the Leal poolside patio.

The Best of Havana Modern Today

Top twenty-five personal favorites in order of fondness. Most are listed in the essential tour book *The Havana Guide: Modern Architecture 1925–1965* by Eduardo Luis Rodríguez.

Note: The building's name is followed by date of construction and architect(s). Addresses are listed according to the Cuban convention with street number or name, building number, cross streets, and district. For example, under the American convention, the address of the Eugenio Leal Residence, entry #2, would be 115 Eighteenth Street between First and Third avenues in the Miramar district.

1. **Havana Riviera Hotel.** 1957, Igor Polevitzky (Polevitzky, Johnson & Associates). Malecón at 1, Vedado.

2. **Eugenio Leal Residence** (now a restaurant). 1957, Eduardo Cañas Abril and Nujim Nepomechie. 18 #115 (between 1 and 3), Miramar.

3. **Nautical Club.** 1953, Max Borges Jr. Terminus of 152, Náutico.

4. **Tropicana Nightclub.** 1951–56, Max Borges Jr. 72 #4505 (between 43 and Línea), Marianao. **Arcos de Cristal** (Crystal Arches). 1951; **Bajo Las Estrellas** (Under the Stars) stage. 1952; **Casino.** 1954; **Cafeteria.** 1956

5. **National Art Schools** (partially abandoned; permission suggested). 1961–65, Ricardo Porro. Cubanacán.

6. **Habana Hilton** (now Habana Libre; altered). 1958, Welton Becket & Associates. Block of L, 23, M and 25, Vedado.

7. **Radiocentro Building: Warner Theater and CMQ Broadcasting** (now Yara Theatre and offices). 1945–47, Junco, Gastón & Domínguez. 23 (between L and M), Vedado.

8. **Solimar Apartments.** 1944, Manuel Copado. Soledad #205 (between San Lázaro and Ánimas), Centro Habana.

9. **Office of the Comptroller** (now Ministry of Interior). 1953, Aquiles Capablanca. Aranguren (at corner of Carlos Manuel de Céspedes), Plaza Civica.

10. **Tomb of Núñez-Gálvez.** 1957, Max Borges Jr. and Enrique Borges. 10 (at corner of D), Cristóbal Colón cemetery, Vedado.

11. **Mausoleum of Havana Reporters Association.** 1957, Arnaldo Mesa. J (at corner of 14), Cristóbal Colón cemetery, Vedado.

12. **Alfred de Schulthess Residence** (now Swiss Ambassador's Residence; behind high wall). 1956, Richard Neutra. 19A #15012 (between 150 and 190), Cubanacán.

13. **Martial Facio Residence** (abandoned, slated for demolition). 1941–43, Enrique Virgilio Pérez. 1 #1802 (at corner of 18), Miramar.

14. **Max Borges Jr. Residence.** 1948–50, Max Borges Jr. 1 #3401 (at corner of 34), Miramar.

15. **Enrique Borges Residence.** 1959, Enrique Borges. 32 #307 (between 1 and 3), Miramar.

16. **Hotel Universitario.** Circa 1955, architect unknown. 17 #111 (between L and M), Vedado.

17. **Medical Building** (now Instituto Cirugia Cardiovascular). 1958, abstract concrete screen by Rolando Lopez Dirube. Paseo (at corner of 17), Vedado.

18. **Retail Store.** Circa 1953, architect unknown. Obispo #259, Habana Vieja.

19. **José Noval Cueto Residence.** 1949, Mario Romañach (Bosch & Romañach). 17A #17409 (between 174 and 190), Cubanácan.

20. **María Melero Residence.** 1940–42, Hermenio Lauderman. 5 #4003 (between 40 and 42), Miramar.

21. **EDA Building** (now branch of Justice Ministry). 1954, Jose Castro Ansa. O #216 (between 23 and 25), Vedado.

22. **Seguro Medical Building.** 1956–58, Antonio Quintana (Quintana, Rubio & Pérez Beato). 23 #201 (at corner of N), Vedado.

23. **Hotel Capri.** 1956, Jose Canaves Ugalde. N and 21, Vedado.

24. **FOCSA Building.** 1954–56, Ernesto Gómez Sampera and Martin Domínguez. Block of 17, M, 15 and N, Vedado.

25. **American Embassy.** 1953, Harrison & Abramovitz. Malecón at Calzada (between L and M), Vedado.

New Year's 1958 and Beyond

"I crapped out."

—Meyer Lansky

On December 31, 1958, following a year of intermittent urban bombings, the failure to rout rebel forces from the mountains, defections by government troops, and the imminent loss of the city of Santa Clara to Che Guevara's forces, President Fulgencio Batista prepared to flee Havana—intentions that he kept to himself, his immediate family, and a handful of close associates.

That evening the owners of Havana's big hotels, nightclubs, and cabarets were anxiously awaiting the New Year's Eve crowds that would fill their tables, dance floors, and casinos. At the Tropicana, festive decorations greeted revelers as the nightclub's two orchestras played popular up-tempo Cuban and American dance numbers. At 11:40 that night, Meyer Lansky's wife, Teddy, danced in the Riviera's elegant Copa Room, not with her husband, but with their Cuban attorney

Eduardo Suarez, while Meyer, alone in his penthouse suite, nursed a painfully swollen knee and a recurring debilitating ulcer. At the elegant Plaza and Sevilla-Biltmore hotels and in the midmarket game rooms of the hotels Deauville and St. Johns, gamblers threw dice and watched the roulette wheels as the clock ticked toward midnight. And at the Hotel Capri, debonair greeter George Raft welcomed in the New Year with his usual "champagne flair."

As confetti rained down and shouts of "Feliz Año Nuevo" punctuated the night, President Batista huddled with senior military and government officials at Camp

RIGHT:
A victorious Castro parades through Havana in January 1959.

Colombia, Havana's army headquarters. Having received confirmation that Santa Clara had fallen and that the country's second city, Santiago de Cuba, was surrounded by Castro's forces, Batista announced to the group, effective immediately, that he was handing power over to a provisional military *junta,* which was to appoint Supreme Court justice Carlos Piedra as the country's new president. Then, swiftly, the former president left the building with a clique of favored military men and political allies for a waiting aircraft already crowded with Batista cronies and their families. The plane's engines fired up and, within minutes, Fulgencio Batista y Zaldívar, the sergeant stenographer who rose to become Cuba's most enduring political puppet master, was gone.

Unlike the dramatic scene in Francis Ford Coppola's *Godfather Part II* where Batista announces his departure with a New Year's ballroom toast followed by a mad rush of Cuban officials, rich tourists, mobsters, and Havana's elite to waiting yachts, it wasn't until well past midnight that the first rumors of Batista's flight actually began circulating in the city. And the news came as a panic-inducing shock to the scores of Batista supporters—policemen, midlevel army officers, businessmen, government officials, and many of the dictator's brutal torturers and informants—left behind to fend for themselves. The clever or the lucky acted quickly to secure last-minute commercial or military flights from Havana on New Year's morning until rebel commanders shut down the airport that afternoon. In the coming days, hundreds of Batistianos who hadn't found a way off the island would be apprehended and, following quick show trials, summarily executed, to the professed outrage of an Eisenhower administration already suspicious of Castro's intentions.

Contrary to initial news reports, neither Meyer Lansky, his brother Jake, Santo Trafficante, Lefty Clark, nor any other members of Havana's gambling syndicate fled Cuba on New Year's Eve or the following day. Although just as stunned as the rest of Cuba by Batista's sudden departure and keenly aware of their status as prime targets of the incoming regime, Havana's gambling kingpins remained behind to protect their investments and, perhaps, negotiate the continued operation of their casinos with the rebel leaders.

As waves of groaning aircraft departed through the night and into New Year's Day, Havana awoke to the smashing of the city's hated parking meters, the sacking of its smaller casinos (at the Plaza, Sevilla-Biltmore, Deauville, and St. Johns), and the looting of the suburban houses of Batista's just-escaped relatives and friends. American newspapers such as the *Los Angeles Times* carried the story of a defiant George Raft who single-handedly held off an angry mob intent on wrecking his Capri casino by standing atop a dice table telling them of his political neutrality " . . . and [that] if they wanted anything they were welcome to take it. But I implored them not to break up the place. I told them I had plenty of food and that I would feed them." Raft said interpreters translated his message to the rebel leaders and they agreed to the feeding idea.

Separate from the localized violence, the city welcomed New Year's Day with mounting relief as recognition that the civil war had finally ended led to ecstatic outpourings of joy with thousands of Habaneros honking horns, joining spontaneous street parades, singing, dancing, and embracing. Havana's bewildered tourists, however, were generally terrified by the turn of events. Many ignored

CLOCKWISE FROM FACING LEFT: Smashing into the Sevilla-Biltmore's casino. Death of a slot machine. A wrecked casino on New Year's Day. Bonfire of the gaming tables. Celebrating as the Centro Gallego Building's casino smolders. Surveying the wreckage of the Hotel Plaza's casino. A policeman takes aim at the Plaza's looters.

embassy instructions to remain in their hotels and attempted to flee the city by crowding the international airport prior to its closure.

From his headquarters in the newly liberated city of Santiago de Cuba in eastern Oriente province, rebel commandant Fidel Castro invoked a general strike and demanded that all looting and violent activity immediately cease. By nightfall a tense calm enveloped the capital city. The following day, Castro appointed the respected lawyer Manuel Urrutia as provisional president. Among Urrutia's first decrees was the immediate closure of Cuba's casinos and the cessation of the national lottery.

For seven restless days Havana awaited Castro's triumphal entry into the city as he slowly made his way along Cuba's central highway from Santiago, stopping at each city along its five-hundred-mile route as euphoric crowds overwhelmed the rebels with adulation. Greeting Castro as a liberator, Cubans eagerly embraced the bearded hero's promise of ending endemic government corruption and celebrated Castro's assurances of untainted national elections, press freedoms, and good relations with the United States. The tumultuous welcome that Habaneros gave Castro and his rebel army upon entering the city on January 8, 1959, was the largest in Cuban history.

With President Urrutia officially inhabiting the presidential palace, Castro and his men chose the Habana Hilton as their provisional headquarters, with the commandant

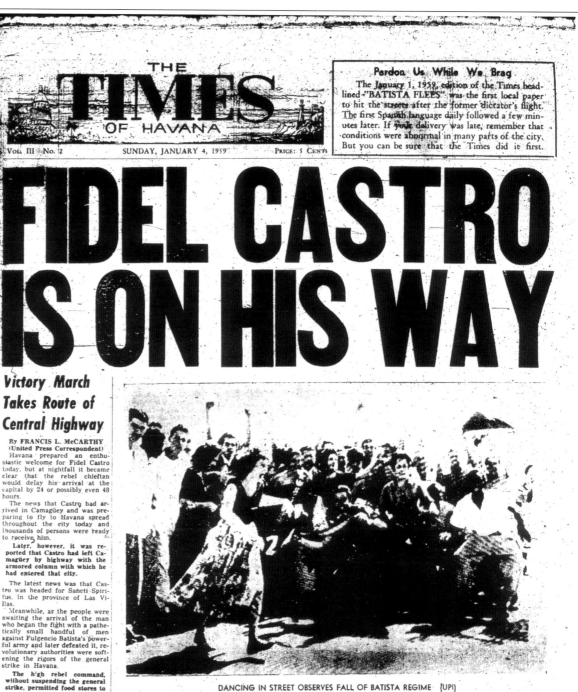

THE TIMES OF HAVANA

Vol. III · No. 12   SUNDAY, JANUARY 4, 1959   Price: 5 Cents

Pardon Us While We Brag

The January 1, 1959, edition of the Times headlined "BATISTA FLEES" was the first local paper to hit the streets after the former dictator's flight. The first Spanish language daily followed a few minutes later. If your delivery was late, remember that conditions were abnormal in many parts of the city. But you can be sure that the Times did it first.

FIDEL CASTRO IS ON HIS WAY

Victory March Takes Route of Central Highway

By FRANCIS L. McCARTHY
(United Press Correspondent)

Havana prepared an enthusiastic welcome for Fidel Castro today, but at nightfall it became clear that the rebel chieftan would delay his arrival at the capital by 24 or possibly even 48 hours.

The news that Castro had arrived in Camagüey and was preparing to fly to Havana spread throughout the city today and thousands of persons were ready to receive him.

Later, however, it was reported that Castro had left Camagüey by highway with the armored column with which he had entered that city.

The latest news was that Castro was headed for Sancti-Spiritus, in the province of Las Villas.

Meanwhile, as the people were awaiting the arrival of the man who began the fight with a pathetically small handful of men against Fulgencio Batista's powerful army and later defeated it, revolutionary authorities were softening the rigors of the general strike in Havana.

The high rebel command, without suspending the general strike, permitted food stores to open two hours a day, permitted civilians to walk through the streets and granted permission to foreign airplanes to land and take off at the Ha-

most difficult stretch of his journey before him. He still must enter the province of Las Villas which, of all the nation's six pro-

largest number of bridges and highways.

This means that if Castro has required 36 hours to march 350

time in each of the cities through which he passes."

Ernesto "Che" Guevara, Argentine rebel commander who had

permitted newspapers to renew publication.

Diego and Guevara also gave permission to civilians to drive

DANCING IN STREET OBSERVES FALL OF BATISTA REGIME (UPI)

FACING:
The *Times of Havana* covers Castro's victory march across Cuba.

BELOW:
Euphoric crowds greet the triumphant rebels.

occupying the hotel's uppermost floors. Castro could not have chosen a more apt spot for the locus of his new regime—the most visible symbol of America's presence in Havana—making plain the nature of the new relationship that would rapidly unfold between the two countries.

Within a few weeks, however, some of the young government's initial edicts, such as the closure of the casinos, resulted in a popular backlash. At the end of January, street protests by several thousand waiters, cooks, bartenders, dealers, performers, janitors, and other employees of Havana's many hotels, nightclubs, and cabarets that had been subsidized by casino profits led Castro to backpedal. Citing concern for the workers' livelihoods, Castro reversed Urrutia's decree and reopened the casinos in February 1959 (but now under close government supervision). However, to the disappointment of all,

Despite the United States government's wary reaction to the rebel victory, official American recognition of Castro's regime had been remarkably swift. Four months after entering Havana, in April 1959, Castro made a triumphal visit to New York City where he was warmly received by the American press, if not by the American government.

LEFT:
Castro's men being fed in the Habana Hilton, which they occupied after taking the city.

perhaps, save Castro and his ideological comrades, the fun-loving tourists failed to return. And why would they? There were other Caribbean resorts eager for the tourist dollar—Bermuda, the Bahamas, Puerto Rico, the Virgin Islands, even Haiti—where revolutionary passions and incendiary anti-American political rhetoric were blissfully absent.

In October 1960, after almost two years of hemorrhaging money, Castro ended the slow death of Havana's hotel/casinos by seizing them from their American and Cuban owners—Lansky, Trafficante, Hilton, and the rest. Commented Meyer Lansky years later of the loss of his beloved Riviera and his final departure from Havana in late 1960, "I crapped out."

However, less than a year later, the tit-for-tat escalation of hostility between the United States and Cuba was already in full bloom. As Castro flirted with the Soviet Union, the American government drastically cut purchases of Cuban sugar (leading to a corresponding increase in Soviet sugar imports). Castro's expropriations of private property led to the United States breaking off diplomatic relations, the American trade embargo, the Bay of Pigs fiasco, and the placement of Soviet missiles in Cuba culminating in the terrifying brinksmanship of the Cuban Missile Crisis.

As an epitaph to the depravities of the Batista era, a joint Soviet-Cuban propaganda film of exceptional power and artistic beauty titled *I Am Cuba* was released in 1964. Depicted in one of the film's vignettes are lecherous, decadent Americans who have come to steal the country's innocence—with "innocence" represented by a young mulatta from Havana's slums. Out of desperation, she is drawn to the hypnotic world of the city's bars and nightclubs, where their illicit charms lead her to a life of prostitution. Ironically, the film was judged a failure by both Soviet and Cuban audiences, the latter of whom apparently did not buy into the movie's melodramatic portrayal of the years preceding the revolution.

Castro's enduring revolution was based upon the promise of equality, education, health care, housing, and basic sustenance for all, backed by a rigid enforcement apparatus. In exchange, Cuba's middle and upper classes were sacrificed as the government expropriated privately owned businesses—from the telephone company to the corner market—leading to the mass exodus of Cuba's professional and merchant classes: its managers, entrepreneurs, shopkeepers, architects, and attorneys. The years since have been difficult for its people and unkind to its built environment.

As the twenty-first century unfolds, it is unclear whether the majority of the city of Havana—its crumbling infrastructure and irreplaceable stock of twentieth-century architecture—can or will be rescued. Or, conversely, will Havana be sacrificed for the immediate gratification of speculative high-rise condominiums and sprawling shopping malls common to cities from Shanghai to Moscow that have experienced abrupt economic transformations? With luck and foresight, perhaps Havana will choose a different path, reclaiming its status as the Pearl of the Antilles without surrendering its soul.

RIGHT:
Debauched Americans in pre-Castro Havana as depicted in the 1964 Soviet–Cuban propaganda film *I Am Cuba.*

FAR RIGHT:
An innocent mulatta seduced by the decadence of Batista's Havana.

Bibliography

Books

Bardach, Ann Louise. *Cuba Confidential: Love and Vengeance in Miami and Havana*. New York: Vintage, 2002.

Berry, Jeff. *Sippin' Safari*. San Jose, California: Club Tiki Press, 2007.

Cepero, Eloy G. *Cuba 1902–1962: A Journey Through Postcards*. Hialeah, Florida: Eloy G. Cepero, 2002.

Chomsky, Aviva, Barry Carr, and Pamela Maria Smorkaloff, editors. *The Cuba Reader: History, Culture, Politics*. Durham and London: Duke University Press, 2003.

Eire, Carlos M. N. *Waiting for Snow in Havana: Confessions of a Cuban Boy*. New York: The Free Press, 2003.

Engels, Hans. *Havana: The Photography of Hans Engels*. Munich: Prestel Verlag, 1999.

Greene, Graham. *Our Man in Havana*. New York: Viking, 1958.

Gutiérrez, Pedro Juan. *Dirty Havana Trilogy*. New York: HarperCollins, 2002.

Hess, Alan. *Googie: Fifties Coffee Shop Architecture*. San Francisco: Chronicle, 1986.

Hitchcock, Henry-Russell. *Latin American Architecture Since 1945*. New York: Museum of Modern Art, 1955.

Jenkins, Gareth, editor. *Havana In My Heart: 75 Years of Cuban Photography*. Chicago: Chicago Review Press, 2002.

Kirsten, Sven. *Tiki Modern*. Köln: Taschen, 2007.

Lacey, Robert. *Little Man: Meyer Lansky and the Gangster Life*. Boston: Little, Brown and Company, 1992.

Lowinger, Rosa and Ofelia Fox. *Tropicana Nights: The Life and Times of the Legendary Cuban Nightclub*. Orlando, Florida: Harcourt, 2005.

Miller, John and Aaron Kenedi, editors. *Inside Cuba: The History, Culture, and Politics of an Outlaw Nation*. New York: Marlowe & Company, 2003.

Moore, Andrew. *Inside Havana*. San Francisco: Chronicle, 2002.

Orovio, Helio. *Cuban Music from A to Z*. Durham, North Carolina: Duke University Press, 2004.

Polidori, Robert. *Havana*. Gotingen, Germany: Steidl, 2001.

Roberts, W. Adolphe. *Havana: The Portrait of a City*. New York: Coward-McCann, 1953.

Rodríguez, Eduardo Luis. *La Habana: Arquitectural del Siglo XX*. Barcelona: Art Blume, S.L., 1998.

Rodríguez, Eduardo Luis. *The Havana Guide: Modern Architecture 1925–1965*. New York: Princeton Architectural Press, 2000.

Rucker, Mark and Peter C. Bjarkman. *Smoke: The Romance and Lore of Cuban Baseball*. New York: Total/Sports Illustrated, 1999.

Ryan, Alan, editor. *The Readers' Companion to Cuba*. San Diego: Harcourt Brace and Company, 1997.

Smith, Julia Llewellyn. *Traveling on the Edge: Journeys in the Footsteps of Graham Greene*. New York: St. Martin's, 2000.

Terry, T. Philip. *Terry's Guide to Cuba*. New York: Houghton Mifflin, 1929.

Thomas, Hugh. *Cuba: The Pursuit of Freedom*. New York: Harper & Row, 1971.

Articles, Documents and Other Sources

"A Game of Casino." *Time*, January 20, 1958.

Anderton, Frances. "In Cuba, Seeds of a Design Renaissance." *New York Times*, October 7, 1999.

"Batista, Aides Flee; Mobs Sacking Havana." *Miami Herald*, January 2, 1959.

"Batista and Regime Flee Cuba; Castro Moving to Take Power; Mobs Riot and Loot in Havana." *New York Times*, January 2, 1959.

"Batista's Bid." *Newsweek*, March 17, 1952.

"Batista Flees Cuba; Rebels in Power." *Los Angeles Times*, January 2, 1959.

Baxter, Kevin. "Religion Under Wraps." *Los Angeles Times*, June 26, 2007.

"Bowman to Build Big Havana Hotel." *New York Times*, January 28, 1923.

Brady, James. "Cuba Before Fidel." *Forbes.com*, September 17, 2006.

Cardona, Joe and Mario de Varona (Directors). "Havana Portrait of Yesteryear." [Film]. Miami: WPBT-TV, 1998.

"Castro to Shut Down Cuba's Lush Casinos." *Los Angeles Times*, January 4, 1959.

Conaway, J. "Papa's Place." *Preservation*, Vol. 59, No. 3 (May/June 2007).

"Counting Batista's Days." *Newsweek*, December 22, 1958.

"Cuba in Dire Straits." *New York Times*, December 31, 1958.

"Cuba Libre." *New York Times*, January 4, 1959.

"Cuba: Peten's Passenger." *Time*, May 15, 1933.

"Cuba: The Vengeful Victory." *Time*, January 26, 1959.

CubaNow.net. The Digital Magazine of Cuban Arts and Culture.

Dickinson, Leon A. "Under Cuban Skies: Splendid Central Highway Makes Picturesque Island Accessible to Cars." *New York Times*, February 21, 1932.

Darling, Henry. "Cuba: Gambling Mecca of the New World." *Cabaret*, December, 1956.

Darling, Henry. "Night Club in the Sky." *Cabaret*, January, 1957.

Fortune, Robert. "Sin – With a Rhumba Beat!" *Stag*, Vol. 1, No. 5, November, 1950.

Friedman, Charles. "Havana's Art Center." *New York Times*, November 20, 1955.

"Gamblers in Cuba Face Dim Future." *New York Times*, January 4, 1959.

Goldberger, Paul. "Bringing Back Havana." *New Yorker*, Vol. 73 January 26, 1998.

"Habana Hilton." *Interiors*, August, 1958.

Havemann, Ernest. "Mobsters Move In On Troubled Havana and Split Gambling Profits with Batista." *Life*, March 10, 1958.

Hemingway, Valerie. "Hemingway's Cuba, Cuba's Hemingway." *Smithsonian*, August, 2007.

"High Wind in Havana." *Time*, February 3, 1958.

Historical Museum of Southern Florida, Research Center, Igor B. Polevitzky collection.

Hubbard, Mrs. W. W. "People's Own Clubs of Havana." *New York Times*, June 1, 1919.

Kalatozov, Mikhail (Director). "Soy Cuba [I Am Cuba]." [Film]. Cuba/USSR: Mosfilm, 1964.

Jewell, Edward Alden. "Modernism in Cuba." *New York Times*, September 7, 1947.

Johnson, Reed. "Mixed Visions of the Future in Post-Fidel Cuba." *Los Angeles Times*, August 20, 2006.

"The Journal of Decorative and Propaganda Arts: Cuba Theme Issue," #22. Miami: Wolfson Foundation of Decorative and Propaganda Arts, 1996.

"The Journal of Decorative and Propaganda Arts: Florida Theme Issue," #23. Miami: Wolfsonian-Florida International University, Wolfson Foundation of Decorative and Propaganda Arts, 1998.

Livermore, Henrietta W. "Cuba Plans to Enhance Her Charms." *New York Times*, September 5, 1926.

Lynch, James. "Cuban Architecture Since the Revolution." *Art Journal*, Vol. 39, No. 2, (Winter, 1979–1980).

"Making Havana a City Beautiful." *New York Times*, February 22, 1920.

Mallin, Jay. "Shanghai Theater: The World's Rawest Burlesque Show." *Cabaret*, September, 1956.

McClure, Rosemary. "Cuba, Suspended in Time." *Los Angeles Times*, January 15, 2006.

Mendoza, Tony. "The Lessons of Bernard Baruch." http://art.osu.edu/faculty/tony/bernard.htm, 1995.

"Mob Figure Takes Fifth in Assassinations Inquiry." *Los Angeles Times*, March 16, 1977.

Passell, Peter. "Forbidden Sun, and Sin, Communist Style." *New York Times*, November 7, 1993.

Perdomo, Ismael (Director). "Cabaret: Los Años Cincuenta La Habana Inventada." [Film]. Habana: Una Produccion de la Oficina Álvarez, Santiago, 2001.

Phillips, R. Hart. "Cuba's Famous 'Playa Azul'." *New York Times*, March 17, 1946.

"Police Free Gambling Czar." *Los Angeles Times*, February 13, 1958.

"Raft's Oratory Saves Casino from Cubans." *Los Angeles Times*, January 6, 1959.

"Rebels Take Over Reins in Havana." *Los Angeles Times*, January 6, 1959.

"Resigned Cubans Expect No Changes." *Los Angeles Times*, December 17, 2006.

Skylar, Richard. "Havana's Shanghai Theater." *Suppressed*, Vol. 4, No. 1, February, 1957.

"Special Report: Cuba." *Cigar Aficionado*, May/June, 2001.

The Steve Allen Show, January 19, 1958. NBC. "Live from the Havana Riviera Hotel, Havana Cuba."

Thackrey Jr., Ted. "Meyer Lansky, Reputed Mob Patriarch, Dies." *Los Angeles Times*, January 16, 1983.

"Thirteen Reported Killed in Havana Riots," *Los Angeles Times*, January 2, 1959.

University of Miami, Cuban Heritage Collection.

Velie, Lester. "Suckers in Paradise: How Americans Lose Their Shirts in Caribbean Gambling Joints." *Saturday Evening Post*, March 28, 1953.

Welton Becket and Associates archives, Los Angeles, California.

Williams, Carol J. "From the Ground Up, Cuba is Crumbling." *Los Angeles Times*, September 19, 2006.

Williams, Carol J. "Ownership in Cuba Becomes Hot Issue." *Los Angeles Times*, September 10, 2006.

Wise, Michael Z. "The Challenge of a Crumbling Havana." *New York Times*, January 14, 1996.

Wolfsonian Collection, Florida International University.

Index

Photo Credits

All images from author's collection

except for the following:

Associated Press: 11, 227 (right), 247 (below left)

Bruce Becket and Associates, Welton Becket archives: 2, 204, 205 (above left, above right), 206, 207, 208 (above right, below right), 209, 210, 211 (above left, above right), 212, 213, 215, 219

Cathy Callahan: 53, 126 (above), 130 (above left, below left, below right)

Rafael Diaz Casas: 135 (right)

Dio Deltoro: 216 (below left)

The Granger Collection, New York: 13, 17 (below left)

Historical Museum of Southern Florida: 184 (above right), 186 (left), 188 (above left), 198 (above left, above right), 199 (above left, below left), 222 (above right)

Sven A. Kirsten: back flap (below), back cover, 7, 19 (far right), 20 (above right), 28 (above), 33, 47 (below left), 51 (above left), 57 (left), 82 (right), 83, 85 (left), 86 (below), 87, 88, 90 (right), 93 (left), 94, 95, 98 (above right), 107, 115 (above), 121, 127 (below right), 128 (above right), 129 (above left), 131 (above), 132 (below), 144 (below right), 154, 156, 157, 183, 185 (above right), 186 (above right), 187, 188 (below left, right), 190, 192, 193 (right),

197 (below right), 198 (below right), 199 (above right, below right), 200, 201, 203, 214 (right), 216 (above right), 217 (above left, below left, right), 224 (above right), 228 (above right), 229 (left), 232 (above right), 234, 236 (left, center), 237 (above left, above right), 240 (below center, below right), 241, 242 (images 1, 2, 3, 5, 6, 11), 243 (images 12, 13, 14, 16, 17, 18, 20, 21, 24)

Library of Congress: 17 (below right)

Vincent Martino Jr.: 82 (left), 176 (above right), 177 (above right), 182 (above right), 186 (below right), 189 (right), 191 (above right, middle right), 193 (above), 196, 221, 222 (below right), 223, 224 (below right), 243 (image 23)

James J. McQuaid: 208 (above left)

Milestone Film & Video: 251

Time & Life Pictures: 181 (above left, middle, right), 175 (above), 194 (left), 224 (left)

University of Miami Libraries, Cuban Heritage Collection: 60 (right), 134 (below), 177 (bottom left), 220 (second from left), 240 (below left), 242 (image 10)

While every effort has been made to find the photographers and copyright holders for the material contained in this book, a few remain uncredited. We welcome information that will help us give proper credit in successive editions.